COLOR FOR
ALL SEASONS

CHIHULY
GARDEN AND GLASS

COLOR FOR ALL SEASONS

FIELD GUIDE

ESSAYS AND
PLANT CHARTS BY
SHANNA JONES &
KAITLIN RYAN

WITH INTRODUCTIONS BY
MICHELLE BUFANO &
RICHARD HARTLAGE

CHIHULY WORKSHOP

INTRODUCTION

ABOUT THE ARTIST

ART IN THE GARDEN

ABOUT THE GARDEN

PLANT CHARTS

APPENDIX

MICHELLE BUFANO

*I want my work to appear like it came from nature, so
that if someone found it on a beach or in the forest, they
might think it belonged there.*

—Dale Chihuly, 1996

Since opening in the spring of 2012, Chihuly Garden and Glass has celebrated the work, and inspirations, of one of the Northwest's mostly highly
regarded artists, Dale Chihuly. Located at Seattle Center, Chihuly Garden and
Glass strives to inspire and engage guests, to leave them wanting to know
more about this region and its artists.

As you walk through Chihuly Garden and Glass, you can see the regional
influences of the Pacific Northwest that have shaped Chihuly's work. You will
witness this inspiration in the Native American baskets and trade blankets of
the Northwest Room, the *Sealife Tower* reflecting his love of the Puget Sound,
and, perhaps most important, his memories of the garden created by his
mother, Viola Chihuly. The variety of shapes and colors evident in both the
Mille Fiori installation and the garden demonstrates the great impact of the
natural elements in his mother's garden on Chihuly's work.

Over the past five decades, Chihuly's career has redefined the way people
perceive and experience glass art. He has pushed the boundaries of the
abstract glass medium by employing gravity and centrifugal force, rather than
just heat and glassblowing tools, to guide his work. In addition to the pieces
themselves, he has reinvented the way art is presented. No longer just vessels
on pedestals, Chihuly's work has taken on architectural form, suspended from

Michelle Bufano, 2016

walls and ceilings. All the while, he continues to exhibit work outside gallery walls. He first experimented with glass outdoors at Pilchuck Glass School, where he often placed the work in vignettes of grass and forest.

Chihuly has said, "I love to juxtapose the man-made and the natural to make people wonder and ask, 'Are they man-made or did they come from nature?'" It's inspiring to see this play out daily at Chihuly Garden and Glass. Our guests are entranced both by Chihuly's artwork, which is integrated with living plants, and by the plants themselves. Working alongside the landscape designer Richard Hartlage, Dale Chihuly created an exceptional synergy of artwork and the splendor of nature, with an ambience unlike that of any garden or exhibition elsewhere: Chihuly's art enhances the unique plant collection while implementing striking colors and forms of the natural world to highlight the art. Winter, spring, summer, or fall, the garden provides those who visit with an experience that is endlessly different.

Michelle Bufano
Executive Director
Chihuly Garden and Glass

RICHARD HARTLAGE

Seattle is one of the most accommodating climates to garden in, so when we began discussing a major permanent outdoor exhibition of Dale Chihuly's work, it made perfect sense to include a garden that would showcase the art and complement the interior galleries. There is also the significant historical context of locating Chihuly Garden and Glass at the Seattle Center, which is a fifty-acre campus and the site of the 1962 World's Fair.

As the project started to come together, we were hired in advance of the architect, Owen Richards Architects (ORA), because of Chihuly's love of gardens. My own history of developing and managing public gardens on both coasts of the United States, as well as my familiarity with the temporary exhibitions that Chihuly Studio has installed around the country, contributed to a dynamic collaboration.

Our mission became the development of an inspiring public garden in Seattle. We were tasked with designing a place that highlighted Chihuly's work while celebrating the lavish array of plants that can be grown in our temperate climate. Seattle is known for its rain, but the secret is that our summers are typically gentle and cool, with low humidity and very little rainfall. Our highest amount of rainfall comes in December, January, and February.

Now, meandering paths lead visitors through the garden, while strategically located rectangular resting places provide areas to admire and study the major pieces of art in the outdoor setting. No matter what time of year you visit, including the winter months, the art is inspiring and there is something in flower. Through careful planning, ongoing plant additions are choreographed to complement the art in form, structure, and flower color.

Richard Hartlage, 2016

The garden's design is based on a rich, natural, and ecological arrangement of plants that mimics nature. The garden is not static; the head gardener, Shanna Jones, continues to work with us to change and evolve it on a daily basis. She is immensely talented and a pleasure to work with. Our own role over time has diminished as we pass on to her and her team our knowledge of the design and vision for the garden.

The garden is a world unto itself, with the iconic Space Needle looming overhead. Regardless of your knowledge and interest in gardens, Chihuly Garden and Glass will delight, inspire, and educate you. It is the perfect accompaniment to Dale Chihuly's world-renowned art and an ever-changing experience for visitors.

Richard Hartlage
Principal and CEO
Land Morphology

DALE CHIHULY

Dale Chihuly, 2016

Born in 1941 in Tacoma, Washington, Dale Chihuly was introduced to glass while studying interior design at the University of Washington. After graduating in 1965, Chihuly enrolled in the first glass program in the country, at the University of Wisconsin. He continued his studies at the Rhode Island School of Design (RISD), where he later established the glass program and taught for more than a decade.

In 1968, after receiving a Fulbright Fellowship, he went to work at the Venini glass factory in Venice. There he observed the team approach to blowing glass, which is critical to the way he works today. In 1971, Chihuly cofounded Pilchuck Glass School in Washington State. With this international glass center, Chihuly has led the avant-garde in the development of glass as a fine art.

His work is included in more than 200 museum collections worldwide. He has been the recipient of many awards, including two fellowships from the National Endowment for the Arts and twelve honorary doctorates.

Chihuly has created more than a dozen well-known series of works, among them, *Cylinders* and *Baskets* in the 1970s; *Seaforms, Macchia, Persians,* and *Venetians* in the 1980s; *Niijima Floats* and *Chandeliers* in the 1990s; and *Fiori* in the 2000s. He is also celebrated for large architectural installations. In 1986, he was honored with a solo exhibition, *Dale Chihuly objets de verre,* at the Musée des Arts Décoratifs, Palais du Louvre, in Paris. In 1995, he began *Chihuly Over Venice,* for which he created sculptures at glass factories in Finland, Ireland, and Mexico, then installed them over the canals and piazzas of Venice.

In 1999, Chihuly started an ambitious exhibition, *Chihuly in the Light of Jerusalem*; more than 1 million visitors attended the Tower of David Museum to view his installations. In 2001, the Victoria and Albert Museum in London curated the exhibition *Chihuly at the V&A.* Chihuly's lifelong fascination for glasshouses has grown into a series of exhibitions within botanical settings, sites that enable the artist to juxtapose monumental, organically shaped sculptural forms with beautiful landscaping, establishing a direct and immediate interaction between nature, art, and environmental light. His *Garden Cycle* began in 2001 at the Garfield Park Conservatory in Chicago. Chihuly exhibited at the Royal Botanic Gardens, Kew, near London, in 2005. He has continued to exhibit at other venues, including the de Young Museum in San Francisco, in 2008; the Museum of Fine Arts, Boston, in 2011; the Montreal Museum of Fine Arts, in 2013; and the Royal Ontario Museum, Toronto, in 2016. Chihuly Garden and Glass, a long-term exhibition, opened at Seattle Center in 2012.

ART
IN THE
GARDEN

Chihuly Garden and Glass, 2012

Cattails and Niijima Floats, 2012

Viola Crystal Tower, 2012

Black Herons, Black Eelgrass, and *Niijima Floats,* installed 2012

Cobalt Fiori, Niijima Floats, and
Double Turquoise Reeds, installed 2012

Citron Icicle Tower and Red Reeds, 2012

Mexican Hat Tower and
Amber Herons, 2012

Neodymium Reeds, 2012

ABOUT
THE
GARDEN

Chihuly Garden and Glass, 2016

ORIGIN OF THE GARDEN

Since opening in 2012, Chihuly Garden and Glass has gained national and international recognition as a major destination and a signature landscape. Before the garden was established, the site was an amusement park known as the Fun Forest, on an asphalt lot. What you see today is the outcome of years of technical planning, an extensive collaboration between designer Richard Hartlage and Dale Chihuly, along with his team at Chihuly Studio, to create a garden setting that highlights the art installed there.

The interior garden is roughly three-quarters of an acre, with green walls and three planted roofs. The total site, which includes the walks, entry canopy, and plantings on the west face of the building, is an acre and a half.

Hartlage designed the pedestrian circulation of curving paths in the garden, along the west side of the Space Needle, and made upgrades to the other three sides of the exhibition space and to the way the project is knitted into the Seattle Center.

CHOREOGRAPHING THE PLANTING DESIGN

With a planting plan drawn up in advance as a guide, workers arranged the plants in collaboration with Chihuly Studio. First, they laid out and planted trees and large-scale shrubs. Then Chihuly Studio placed mock-ups of the art, to evaluate compositions of the art and plants. In the next wave of activity, the team planted midsize shrubs and large perennials and replaced the mock-ups with the glass art. Daily assessments of the plantings and art installation started at six o'clock in the morning and continued until sunset, so that the team could see the impact of sunlight and shadows throughout the day. After final approval of the glass compositions, workers completed the art installations and garden setting with the planting of the smallest flora.

With a discerning eye, the team made all this happen at breakneck speed, despite an uncountable number of changes. In the end, the revisions produced a simpatico interaction between art and garden, resulting in the most inspiring effects.

The plantings play a supporting role to the art. For example, trees enclose the garden. A collection of broad-leaved trees such as Teddy Bear and Bracken's Brown Beauty southern magnolias and various needled evergreens like hinoki cypress and dwarf western cedar screen out the busy Seattle Center scene. At the same time, this simple perimeter creates an appropriate backdrop for the art. In addition, groves of trees planted throughout the garden provide scale and establish themes for the lower plantings.

The garden is also organized around a series of color schemes that correspond to colors of the art. The southern portion of the garden is planted in blues and other cool colors, while the northern portion features primarily warm colors. The east side of the Glasshouse is planted with woodland and shade-loving plants.

Architectural model of
Glasshouse and garden, 2011

Chihuly Garden and Glass
under construction, 2011

ADVANCE PLANNING

Plants were acquired from eight states, the farthest afield being Georgia, the source of the Teddy Bear magnolias. We ordered these trees a year in advance to ensure availability. Oregon suppliers started growing the 4,500 plugs of black mondo grass—actually, a flowering plant—that surround the *Pacific Sun* two years prior to planting, to ensure both quantity and quality. During construction, the entire area of the garden was excavated and new soil was added to an average depth of two feet.

TREES

Careful study of the groves of trees shows a wide variety: for example, coral bark and paperbark maples around Chihuly's *Red Reeds*, dogwoods and honey locusts along the east side of the Glasshouse, Stewartias (related to camellias) and dove trees in the southern part of the garden. The Sonoma dove tree grows in very few places in the United States; this Chinese native has large white bracts (particular types of leaves) in April and early May that look like white doves or handkerchiefs covering the tree. These trees are rare and profoundly beautiful.

PERENNIALS AND SHRUBS

Larger-scale perennials and shrubs are planted with spring ephemerals such as primroses, anemones, and bulbs. They are designed to change daily throughout the growing season, so a visitor will never experience the garden the same way on any visit. Pansies, violas, and ornamental kales and cabbages are planted among the perennial and permanent plantings for floral interest in the winter and early spring. In the mild Seattle Zone 8B climate, these plants flower all winter long, with a crescendo in March and April.

Pacific Sun, 2011,
installed 2012

Red Reeds (detail), 2012, and
Arctic Fire red twig dogwood

BULBS

In this complex planting, bulbs serve as the real workhorses. The bulk of the herbaceous perennials bloom in summer and fall. When thinking about bulbs, it's easy to consider only tulips and daffodils. But countless other bulb species succeed and multiply over time. One of the garden's favorite bulb displays is the softball-size allium, which blooms en masse in the teardrop bed. Tulips have been added only recently. Complex hybrid tulips are not bred to succeed year after year, so tulips offer an opportunity to change colors from year to year. A diminutive species that was a favorite of Thomas Jefferson's, the woodland tulip, or *Tulipa sylvestris*, is tough, elegant, and durable, returning annually for decades; its beautiful straw-yellow head complements the blue glass that it nods among. The individual garden beds create a series of memorable moments that make every time a unique experience, whether a person visits only once or every week.

Chihuly floribunda roses on green roof *(top)*; green walls with evergreen clematis *(bottom)*

GREEN ROOFS

The garden includes three green, or planted, roofs, with soil depths ranging between twelve and sixteen inches. All of them can be seen when looking down from the west side of the Space Needle. There is the planted roof above the main entry, the one over the Chandelier Walkway, and another atop the vestibule between the Exhibition Hall and the Glasshouse. They are all planted with a mix of shrubs, perennials, and bulbs. The most notable plant is the creamy orange rose named in the artist's honor: the Chihuly rose. During the summer months, it can be seen flowering above the Chandelier Walkway.

GREEN WALLS

Green walls cover both the east and west faces of the Exhibition Hall. The metal trellis system, planted with more than a dozen and a half different vines, will eventually cloak the building entirely in foliage. The team used evergreen climbing hydrangeas and clematis, honeysuckles, trumpet vines, and many more. The Exhibition Hall, which

June-blooming perennials and *Cobalt Reeds and Fiori* (detail), installed 2012

contains the galleries, is nearly as long as a football field, but the vines make the building seem to disappear. The walls meld into the Seattle Center and provide a simple green backdrop for the garden and art.

SEASONAL INTEREST

The complex arrangements and combinations of plants mimic scenes found in nature. In this system of ecological planting, diverse plants arranged naturalistically and planted very closely together provide a succession of interests and color. In most areas of the garden, any square foot of ground is planted for a minimum of five changes in color and flowering over the course of the growing season.

Not all of the garden's plants are included in this guide; nearly 300 different kinds of plants grow here. Among them, more than 30,000 bulbs delight visitors year-round.

The garden is not static; it changes over time. Whenever you visit, you will see something new to delight you. Thanks to careful consideration, every plant is woven together with its neighbors, providing foreground, setting, and backdrop to the glass art by Dale Chihuly.

COLOR FOR
ALL SEASONS

SPRING

SUMMER

FALL

WINTER

GARDEN MAP

AREAS & INSTALLATIONS

1 Pacific Sun
Neodymium Herons
Tiger Marlins

2 Cobalt Reeds and Fiori
Double Turquoise Reeds

3 Mexican Hat Tower
Amber Herons
Green Hornets and Gold Waterdrops

4 Neodymium Reeds and Seal Pups
Cattails and Niijima Floats

5 Citron Icicle Tower
Cattails and Niijima Floats
Red Reeds

6 Viola Crystal Tower
Black Herons, Black Eelgrass, and Niijima Floats
Black Saguaros
Grey and White Eelgrass and Niijima Floats
Turquoise Trumpets

7 Perimeter

8 Green Roofs

9 Arbor

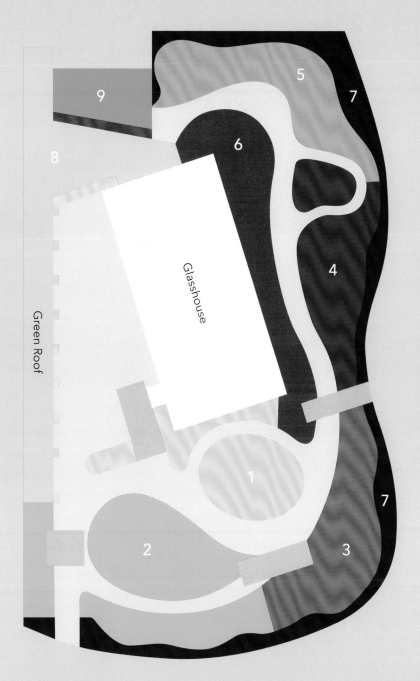

Glasshouse

Green Roof

5

7

9

8

6

4

1

2

3

7

7

BULBS, CORMS, RHIZOMES, AND TUBERS

Allium amplectens 'Graceful'	Graceful ornamental onion	2
Allium giganteum 'Globemaster'	Globemaster ornamental onion	2
Allium nigrum	black garlic	6
Allium schubertii	tumbleweed onion, firework ornamental oinion	6
Allium sphaerocephalon	drumstick ornamental onion	2
Alstroemeria 'Inca Ice'	Peruvian lily	5
Anemone blanda 'Blue Star'	Blue Star Grecian windflower	2
Anemone blanda 'White Splendour'	White Splendour Grecian windflower	2
Anemone coronaria 'Mr. Fokker'	poppy anemone, windflower	2
Arisaema nepenthoides	Jack-in-the-Pulpit, cobra lily	6
Arisaema ringens	Jack-in-the-Pulpit, Japanese cobra lily	6
Arum italicum 'Froggy Bottom'	orange candleflower	4
Arum italicum 'White Winter'	White Winter candleflower	4
Brodiaea 'Pink Diamond'	Pink Diamond fool's onion	1
Brodiaea 'Queen Fabiola'	**Queen Fabiola fool's onion**	2
Camassia leichtlinii 'Caerulea'	**Leichtlin's camass**	4
Chionodoxa gigantea	glory of the snow	2 3
Corydalis curviflora var. *rosthornii* 'Blue Heron'	Blue Heron fumewort	3 5
Corydalis solida 'Beth Evans'	Beth Evans fumewort	9
Crocosmia 'Emily McKenzie'	Emily McKenzie crocosmia	5
Crocosmia 'Little Redhead'	Little Redhead crocosmia	8
Crocus 'Lilac Beauty'	Lilac Beauty crocus	2 3
Crocus tommassinianus	Tommasini's crocus	2 3
Cyclamen coum 'Pewter Leaf Forms'	Persian cyclamen, winter-blooming cyclamen	4
Erythronium 'Pagoda'	trout lily, dog tooth violet	4
Fritillaria meleagris	snake's head fritillary	6
Galanthus elwesii	giant snowdrop	4 6
Ipheion uniflorum	spring starflower	2 4
Iris 'Canyon Snow'	**Pacific coast iris**	2
Iris germanica 'Clarence'	German bearded iris	2 8
Leucojum autumnalis	autumn snowflake	2
Lilium lancifolium 'Splendens'	tiger lily	4
Lilium regale 'Album'	regal lily	5
Lilium ssp. 'Alchemy'	oriental-trumpet lily	5
Muscari latifolium	grape hyacinth	6

BULBS, CORMS, RHIZOMES, AND TUBERS

Scientific name	Common name	Map
Narcissus bulbocodium 'Golden Bells'	hoop petticoat daffodil	1 2 3
Narcissus 'Suzy'	Suzy daffodil	8
Narcissus 'Thalia'	Thalia daffodil	4
Scilla siberica 'Spring Beauty'	Siberian squill	2
Sisyrinchium striatum	pale yellow-eyed grass	2
Tulipa sylvestris	woodland tulip	4
Zantedeschia hybrid	calla lily	3

FERNS

Scientific name	Common name	Map
Asplenium scolopendrium	Hart's tongue fern	4 6
Athyrium filix-femina	**common lady fern**	4
Blechnum chilense	Chilean hard fern	6
Blechnum penna-marina 'Nana'	alpine water fern	4
Cyrtomium fortunei	holly fern	9
Dryopteris wallichiana	Wallich's wood fern	4 6 9
Osmunda regalis	royal fern	4
Polystichum polyblepharum	Japanese tassel fern	4 6

GRASSES

Scientific name	Common name	Map
Carex testacea	orange New Zealand sedge	6
Hakonechloa macra 'Aureola'	gold-leaved Japanese forest grass	4 5
Liriope spicata	lily turf	7
Ophiopogon planiscapus 'Nigrescens'	black mondo grass	1 6
Pennisetum alopecuroides 'Hameln'	dwarf fountain grass	7

PERENNIALS

Scientific name	Common name	Map
Abutilon × hybridum 'Nabob'	climbing flowering maple	9
Abutilon megapotamicum 'Kentish Belle'	Kentish Belle climbing abutilon	5
Abutilon 'Tiger Eye'	flowering maple	5
Acaena inermis 'Purpurea'	purple sheep's burr	2 3
Acaena saccaticupula 'Blue Haze'	New Zealand burr	2 3
Acanthus spinosus	dwarf bear's breeches	1 2
Agastache 'Blue Boa'	hummingbird mint	8
Arisarum proboscideum	mouse plant	4

Native plants of the Pacific Northwest are in bold.

PERENNIALS

Botanical name	Common name	
Aruncus aethusifolius	dwarf goat's beard	6
Aruncus dioicus	goat's beard	6
Asarum splendens	Chinese wild ginger	4 6
Aster cordifolius 'Avondale'	wood aster	8
Aster lateriflorus 'Prince'	Prince calico aster	4 6
Astilboides tabularis (a.k.a. Rodgersia tabularis)	astilboides	6
Beesia calthifolia	beesia	6
Beesia deltophylla	beesia	9
Cardamine pratensis 'Flore-pleno'	double cuckoo flower	6
Chrysanthemum 'Dixter Orange'	Dixter Orange chrysanthamum	8
Dactylorhiza fuchsii 'Bressingham Bonus'	meadow orchid	4
Echinacea 'Green Jewel'	Green Jewel coneflower	2
Epimedium 'Amber Queen'	Amber Queen barrenwort	4
Epimedium 'Domino'	Domino barrenwort	3
Epimedium grandiflorum 'Lilafee'	Lilafee barrenwort	4
Epimedium × versicolor 'Cherry Tart'	Cherry Tart barrenwort	5
Eryngium 'Sapphire Blue'	Sapphire Blue sea holly	2 3
Fuchsia magellanica 'Aurea'	Aurea fuchsia	4
Fuchsia magellanica 'Hawkshead'	white hardy fuchsia	6
Fuchsia 'Mrs. Popple'	Mrs. Popple fuchsia	7
Gentiana acaulis 'Maxima'	trumpet gentian	2
Geranium × cantabrigiense 'St. Ola'	St. Ola cranesbill	2 6
Geranium 'Rozanne'	Rozanne cranesbill	2
Geum 'Totally Tangerine'	Totally Tangerine geum	4
Helleborus × ballardiae 'Cinnamon Snow'	Cinnamon Snow Lenten rose	6
Helleborus × ballardiae 'Pink Frost'	Pink Frost Lenten rose	6
Helleborus × ericsmithii 'Silver Moon'	Silver Moon Lenten rose	6
Helleborus × hybridus 'Black Diamond'	Black Diamond Lenten rose	2
Helleborus × hybridus 'White Pearl'	White Pearl Lenten rose	6
Helleborus niger 'Josef Lemper'	Josef Lemper Christmas rose	6
Hemerocallis 'Breathless Beauty'	scarlet daylily	4
Heuchera 'Obsidian'	Obsidian coral bells	7
Heuchera 'Plum Pudding'	Plum Pudding coral bells	7
Lavandula angustifolia 'Hidcote'	English lavender	2
Pachyphragma macrophyllum	pachyphragma	2 2
Perovskia atriplicifolia	Lacey Blue Russian sage	8
Phormium 'Sundowner'	Sundowner New Zealand flax	7

PERENNIALS

Phormium tenax 'Dusky Chief'	Dusky Chief New Zealand flax	1
Phygelius aequalis 'Moonraker'	cape fuchsia	3
Podophyllum pleianthum	giant mayapple	4
Primula 'Chartreuse'	Chartreuse primrose	2
Primula 'Desert Sunset'	Desert Sunset primrose	6
Primula 'Gilded Ginger'	Gilded Ginger primrose	6
Primula 'Harbour Lights'	Harbour Lights primrose	5
Primula × juliana 'Jay Jay'	Jay Jay primrose	3
Primula 'Little Egypt'	Little Egypt primrose	5
Primula 'Midnight'	Midnight primrose	2
Primula 'Paris 90'	Paris 90 primrose	2
Primula sieboldii 'Late Snow'	Late Snow Japanese primrose	2 3
Primula sieboldii 'Pastel Pink'	Pastel Pink Japanese primrose	2
Primula 'Sorbet'	Sorbet primrose	2
Primula 'Spice Shades'	Spice Shades primrose	6
Ranunculus ficaria 'Solomon's White'	lesser celandine	3
Rumex sanguineus	red-veined dock, bloody dock	4 6
Salvia greggii 'Red Velvet'	Red Velvet Texas sage	6
Santolina chamaecyparissus 'Pretty Carroll'	cotton lavender	3
Saxifraga × geum 'Dentata'	toothed saxifrage	2
Sedum acre 'Aureum'	Aureum sedum	3 6
Sedum rupestre 'Angelina'	Angelina sedum	5 6
Sedum sediforme 'Turquoise Tails'	Turquoise Tails sedum	3 6
Sempervivum arachnoideum 'Cobweb Buttons'	Cobweb Buttons Hen and Chicks	3 6
Sempervivum tectorum 'Royal Ruby'	Royal Ruby Hen and Chicks	3 6
Sempervivum tectorum 'Sunset'	Sunset Hen and Chicks	3 6
Tricyrtis hirta 'Miyazaki'	Miyazki toad lily	2 6
Verbena bonariensis	purple top verbena	2 3

SHRUBS

Aucuba japonica 'Rozannie'	Rozannie aucuba	2
Berberis × gladwynnensis 'William Penn'	William Penn barberry	7
Callicarpa 'Profusion'	Profusion beautyberry	2
Camellia sasanqua 'Yuletide'	Yuletide camellia	5 7
Chaenomeles speciosa 'Scarlet Storm'	flowering quince	5
Cornus sericea 'Arctic Fire'	Arctic Fire red twig dogwood	5

Native plants of the Pacific Northwest are in bold.

SHRUBS

Botanical name	Common name	Map
Corylus avellana 'Contorta'	Harry Lauder's walking stick	1
Cotoneaster dammeri	Bearberry Cotoneaster	8
Daphne genkwa	lilac daphne	2
Daphne × transatlantica 'Summer Ice'	Summer Ice Caucasian daphne	7
Dichroa febrifuga	Chinese quinine	4 7
Edgeworthia chrysantha	rice paper shrub	2
Fatshedera lizei	tree ivy	7
Fatsia japonica	fatsia, Japanese fatsia	4 9
Fothergilla gardenii	dwarf witchalder, dwarf fothergilla	5
Hamamelis japonica 'Shibamichi Red'	Japanese witch hazel	5
Hydrangea macrophylla ssp. serrata 'Bluebird'	Bluebird lacecap hydrangea	2 4 6
Hydrangea macrophylla ssp. serrata 'Blue Deckle'	Blue Deckle lacecap hydrangea	3 4
Hydrangea macrophylla ssp. serrata 'Yae-No-Amacha'	Yae-No-Amacha lacecap hydrangea	4
Hydrangea paniculata 'Limelight'	Limelight panicle hydrangea	2
Hydrangea quercifolia 'Pee Wee'	oakleaf hydrangea	6
Hydrangea serrata 'Tiny Tuff Stuff'	dwarf mountain hydrangea	2
Lonicera nitida	boxleaf honeysuckle	2 8
Lonicera pileata	privet honeysuckle	2 6 7
Mahonia japonica	Japanese mahonia	4 6
Pieris japonica 'Brouwer's Beauty'	Brouwer's Beauty lily-of-the-valley shrub	6
Pieris japonica 'Prelude'	Prelude lily-of-the-valley shrub	1 2 9
Pittosporum tobira 'Wheeler's Dwarf'	Japanese mock orange	1
Podocarpus lawrencei 'Blue Gem'	alpine plum yew	5
Prunus laurocerasus 'Mount Vernon'	Mount Vernon cherry laurel	7
Rhododendron 'Black Sport'	Black Sport rhododendron	6
Rhododendron 'Cunningham White'	Cunningham White rhododendron	3 6 7
Rhododendron 'Dreamland'	Dreamland rhododendron	2 4 6
Rhododendron 'Ramapo'	Ramapo rhododendron	2
Rosa floribunda 'Chihuly'	Chihuly floribunda rose	2
Rosa 'Icy Drift'	Icy Drift carpet rose	2
Sambucus nigra 'Black Lace'	Black Lace elderberry	2
Sarcococca hookeriana var. humilis	dwarf sweetbox	9
Schefflera delavayi	Delavay's schefflera	9
Viburnum plicatum f. tomentosum 'Mariesii'	Marie's doublefile viburnum	3 5 6

TREES

Botanical name	Common name	Locations
Acer griseum	paperbark maple	4 6
Acer palmatum 'Dissectum Atropurpureum'	red weeping cut-leaf Japanese maple	2 3
Acer palmatum 'Sango Kaku'	coral bark Japanese maple	3 4 5 7 8
Acer shirasawanum 'Aureum'	golden full moon maple	2
Chamaecyparis lawsoniana 'Oregon Blue'	**Oregon Blue Lawson's cypress**	7
Chamaecyparis nootkatensis 'Glauca Pendula'	**weeping Alaskan cedar**	7
Chamaecyparis obtusa 'Gracilis'	slender hinoki cypress	7
Cornus rutgersensis 'Celestial'	Celestial dogwood	1 6
Cryptomeria japonica 'Black Dragon'	Black Dragon Japanese cedar	6
Davidia involucrata 'Sonoma'	Sonoma dove tree, handkerchief tree	2 6
Gleditsia triacanthos var. inermis 'Shademaster'	Shademaster thornless honeylocust	4
Magnolia grandiflora 'Bracken's Brown Beauty'	Bracken's Brown Beauty magnolia	7
Magnolia grandiflora 'Teddy Bear'	Teddy Bear magnolia	7
Picea pungens 'Glauca Pendula'	weeping Colorado blue spruce	3
Sciadopitys verticillata 'Wintergreen'	Wintergreen umbrella pine	3 7
Stewartia pseudocamellia	Japanese stewartia	2
Taxus baccata 'Repandens'	spreading English yew	2 4 5
Taxus cuspidata 'Nana'	dwarf Japanese yew	1 6
Thuja plicata 'Atrovirens'	western red cedar	5 7

VINES

Botanical name	Common name	Locations
Akebia quinata	chocolate vine, fiveleaf akebia	8
Clematis 'Arabella'	Arabella ground cover clematis	1 2 6
Clematis armandii	evergreen clematis	7 8
Clematis ternifolia 'Sweet Autumn'	Sweet Autumn clematis	9
Holboellia coriacea 'Cathedral Gem'	Cathedral Gem sausage vine	1
Holboellia coriacea 'China Blue'	China Blue sausage vine	1
Hydrangea integrifolia	evergreen climbing hydrangea	9
Lonicera periclymenum 'Serotina'	Serotina honeysuckle	2 8
Lonicera sempervirens 'Major Wheeler'	Major Wheeler trumpet honeysuckle	8
Trachelospermum jasminoides	confederate jasmine	9
Wisteria floribunda 'Cypress Blue'	Japanese wisteria	9
Wisteria macrostachya 'Aunt Dee'	Kentucky wisteria	9

Native plants of the Pacific Northwest are in bold.

PLANT
HIGHLIGHTS
by Month

JANUARY
Ornamental Kale
Pansies
Violas
Cyclamen
Giant Snowdrop
Helleborus
Beautyberry
Yuletide Camellia
Magnolia

FEBRUARY
Ornamental Kale
Pansies
Violas
Anemone
Crocus
Cyclamen
Giant Snowdrop
Siberian Squill
Helleborus
Primroses
Mahonia
Witch Hazel
Magnolia

MARCH
Ornamental Kale
Pansies
Violas
Anemone
Crocus
Cyclamen
Giant Snowdrop
Jack-in-the-Pulpit

MARCH
Siberian Squill
Tulip
Helleborus
Primroses
Chinese Quince
Daphne
Edgeworthia
Mahonia
Witch Hazel
Evergreen Clematis

APRIL
Anemone
Crocus
Cyclamen
Daffodils
Giant Snowdrop
Jack-in-the-Pulpit
Siberian Squill
Tulip
Ajuga
Geum
Helleborus
Primroses
Chinese Quince
Daphne
Edgeworthia
Mahonia
Witch Hazel
Evergreen Clematis

MAY
Summer Annuals
Allium

Annuals
Bulbs
Perennials
Shrubs
Trees
Vines

MAY

- Iris
- Jack-in-the-Pulpit
- Columbine
- Geranium
- Geum
- Giant May Apple
- Goat's Beard
- Abutilon
- Chihuly Rose
- Elderberry
- Rhododendrons
- Viburnum
- Celestial Dogwood
- Arabella Clematis
- Wisteria

JUNE

- Summer Annuals
- Brodiaea
- Jack-in-the-Pulpit
- Acanthus
- Astilboides
- Calla Lily
- Fuchsia
- Heuchera
- Meadow Orchid
- Salvia
- Satin Flower
- Sea Holly
- Abutilon
- Carpet Rose
- Daphne
- Hydrangeas
- Magnolia

JUNE

- Stewartia
- Umbrella Pine
- Arabella Clematis
- Wisteria

JULY

- Summer Annuals
- Lilies
- Acanthus
- Astilboides
- Cape Fuchsia
- Echinacea
- Fuchsia
- Geranium
- Geum
- Ligularia
- Salvia
- Sea Holly
- Sempervivum
- Toad Lily
- Abutilon
- Carpet Rose
- Hydrangeas
- Passionflower

AUGUST

- Summer Annuals
- Arum
- Crocosmia
- Echinacea
- Geranium
- Salvia
- Sedum
- Sempervivum

AUGUST

- Toad Lily
- Abutilon
- Carpet Rose
- Fuchsia
- Hydrangeas
- Climbing
  Monkshood

SEPTEMBER

- Summer Annuals
- Crocosmia
- Echinacea
- Geranium
- Salvia
- Sedum
- Sempervivum
- Toad Lily
- Abutilon
- Carpet Rose
- Daphne
- Fuchsia
- Hydrangeas
- Sweet Autumn
  Clematis

OCTOBER

- Ornamental Kale
- Pansies
- Violas
- Asters
- Geranium
- Salvia
- Abutilon
- Beautyberry

OCTOBER

- Carpet Rose
- Viburnum
- Japanese Maples
- Stewartia
- Tree Ivy

NOVEMBER

- Ornamental Kale
- Pansies
- Violas
- Asters
- Abutilon
- Beautyberry
- Carpet Rose
- Viburnum
- Yuletide Camellia
- Japanese Maples
- Paperbark Maple

DECEMBER

- Ornamental Kale
- Pansies
- Violas
- Beautyberry
- Yuletide Camellia
- Japanese Maples
- Magnolias
- Paperbark Maple

GARDEN MAINTENANCE

BY SHANNA JONES & KAITLIN RYAN

When the glass art and plants combine into a single statement, something magical happens. As a color moves through the garden from a group of reeds to a mass of spruce and down to a ground cover sedum, it carries one's eyes naturally through the space. Forms are contrasted and mimicked between the plants and the art, along with texture and color. It leaves the viewer wondering if, at first glance, an object is man-made or from nature.

These are the feelings, thoughts, and inspirations we aim to protect. As we prune the rhododendrons, plant summer color, and even deadhead the roses, our goal is always the same: to maintain the garden's appearance as if it naturally grows seamlessly around the art. That being said, we put a tremendous amount of effort into maintaining an effortless look.

Chihuly Garden and Glass garden team: Shanna Jones, Nick Tritt, and Kaitlin Ryan *(left to right)*

Garden team member Erika Langley cutting back ferns

DAILY MAINTENANCE

The garden team at Chihuly Garden and Glass gets to work every morning just as the sun is coming up. This allows a maximum number of daylight hours before we open, to accomplish any larger tasks such as fertilizing, repairing irrigation, transplanting, dividing, doing major planting, or pruning. Sometimes you may find our head gardener out in the garden even earlier, sporting a headlamp!

Each morning, one of the gardeners oversees a check of all our container plantings. We have close to forty, so it's no quick task. While one person hand-waters those pots, another is leaf-blowing all our interior and exterior pathways. Every day, plants in bloom are deadheaded, beds are checked for weeds, insect and disease activity is monitored. All tasks are logged in order for us to best plan for both the near and the more distant future.

Our green screen, located on the south side of the garden, is the trellis system for many perennial and annual vines and also leads up to three sections of roof gardens. While only one of these three beds is visible to our guests, all the beds are easily seen when looking down from the top of our neighbor, the Space Needle. It is important that this area is maintained in the same regard as our ground-level garden. The roses, irises, alliums, and honeysuckle shrubs growing above are all maintained on a regular basis. The roof gardens are constantly monitored for weeds, for appearance's sake as well as to minimize weed seeds that may travel down to ground level.

ORGANIC GARDENING

We practice organic gardening whenever possible. Weekly, we complete the three-day process to brew compost tea. It's applied to our trees and shrubs to give them the extra boost of nutrients they crave. The garden is tightly planted in an urban setting, so our plants appreciate any extra boosts we can give them. In addition, once a week we collect the spent coffee grounds from our café to amend the soil around our acid-loving plants such as hydrangeas, rhododendrons, and yews. These coffee grounds help to slowly lower our soil pH, which is why our hydrangea blooms are such a beautiful soft blue.

PRUNING

Pruning is done throughout the year based on the needs of each plant. Winter is the best time to prune most of our conifers, along with our maples. In the early spring, we give our red twig dogwoods a hard pruning to limit their size and encourage new growth, which has the best color. In the late spring, once the rhododendrons finish blooming, they are pruned before they begin to form the next year's flower buds. In the summer, we monitor the growth of the plants. Art can quickly become hidden by foliage during the growing season. We prune to maintain sight lines without disturbing the natural growth habits of our plants.

PREPARING FOR WINTER

In the fall, we begin to prepare our perennials for dormancy. This is the season the garden goes through the biggest transition. As we cut back perennial plants such as our forest grass and our hardy geraniums, we fill in any gaps with thousands of pansies and violas and hundreds of ornamental kale. Our desire is that no one visits the garden on an off day. We plan our work to transition smoothly, leaving no large gaps and no windows without color. This is also the time of the year when thousands of spring-blooming bulbs are planted. The garden team uses a bulb auger attachment on a hand drill to speed up this process, but it is still a time-consuming task.

Working to maintain the garden at Chihuly Garden and Glass is a unique challenge, unlike working in any other garden. Every day in the garden is different. Even our routine tasks are broken up by new requirements. How we move through the garden is not usually by the most direct path. When we prune the shrubs is not always set in stone. To keep the garden looking spectacular no matter what time of year requires intensive planning, communication, and excellent teamwork.

Robin perched on *Black Eelgrass* (detail), 2012

MAINTENANCE
by Month

JANUARY

- Prune Thujas
- Prune Chihuly Roses
- Mulching
- Tilling
- Fertilize Annuals
- Fertilize Primroses
- Clean Tools

FEBRUARY

- Prune Deciduous Trees
- Prune Cryptomeria
- Prune *Chamaecyparis*
- Prune Magnolias
- Prune Wisteria
- Prune Elderberry
- Prune Aucuba
- Mulching
- Tilling
- Apply Corn Gluten Meal
- Fertilize Primroses
- Fertilize Annuals
- Spring Planning
- Order Summer Annuals
- Northwest Flower & Garden Show

MARCH

- Prune Limelight Hydrangeas
- Prune Dogwoods
- Fertilize Annuals
- Fertilize Primroses
- Apply Sluggo
- Turn Irrigation On
- Irrigation Maintenance
- Summer Planning

APRIL

- Planting Summer Annuals
- Prune Carpet Roses
- Prune Pieris
- Prune Quince
- Prune Fatsia
- Remove Spent Bulb Foliage
- Apply Feather Meal
- Apply Greensand
- Apply Alfalfa Meal to Roses
- Apply Seaweed Fertilizer
- Fertilize Annuals
- Apply Azomite to Annuals
- Apply Sluggo

- Planting
- Pruning
- Cutting/Removing
- Mulching/Tilling
- Fertilizing
- Irrigation
- Other

APRIL

Ladybug Release

Spring Bloom Event

MAY

Planting Summer Annuals

Planting Summer Containers

Prune Mahonias

Prune Umbrella Pine

Prune Camellias

Prune Yews

Clean Hellebores

Remove Spent Bulb Foliage

Apply Alfalfa Meal to Roses

Apply Seaweed Fertilizer

Fertilize Annuals

Apply Azomite to Annuals

Compost Tea

Apply Sluggo

Summer Planning

JUNE

Prune Pittosporum

Prune Viburnums

JUNE

Prune Fothergilla

Prune Rhododendrons

Remove Spent Bulb Foliage

Apply Alfalfa Meal to Roses

Apply Seaweed Fertilizer

Fertilize Annuals

Compost Tea

Irrigation Maintenance

JULY

Cut Back Irises

Remove Spent Bulb Foliage

Apply Seaweed Fertilizer

Fertilize Annuals

Compost Tea

Apply Feather Meal

Apply Alfalfa Meal to Roses

AUGUST

Fertilize Annuals

Fall Planning

Order Fall Bulbs

AUGUST

Order Winter Annuals

SEPTEMBER

Cut Back Fountain Grass

Leaf Removal

Cut Back Sea Holly

Irrigation Maintenance

OCTOBER

Planting Fall/Winter Annuals

Planting Winter Containers

Prune Hydrangea *macrophylla*, *quercifolia*, and *serrata* species

Cut Back Forest Grass

Cut Back Geraniums

Leaf Removal

Fertilize Annuals

Apply Azomite to Annuals

Begin Fertilizing Primroses

NOVEMBER

Planting Bulbs

Mulching

Tilling

Fertilize Annuals and Primroses

Blow Out Irrigation

Winter and Holiday Planning

DECEMBER

Mulching

Tilling

Fertilize Annuals and Primroses

SUSTAINABILITY IN THE GARDEN

BY SHANNA JONES & KAITLIN RYAN

At Chihuly Garden and Glass, being "green" is in our nature. We were designed to be sustainable and reduce our negative impacts on our environment. Sustainability is in mind with everything we do as an organization. The garden is a focal point for many of our sustainability practices. These practices help us to enhance the quality of life for our community, provide economic viability in the long term, stress productivity, encourage a full-circle mentality, and enrich the environmental quality and the resource base from which our nutrients are derived.

The establishment of Chihuly Garden and Glass created a green space, transforming a once vacant concrete lot into a lush habitat for vegetation and wildlife. The building itself was repurposed using recycled, sustainable, and impact-reducing materials. Elements of the construction are energy efficient and cost-effective. This approach to designing the exhibition set the organization up for continued success as a sustainable and environmentally mindful operation. Chihuly Garden and Glass is a silver-level LEED (Leadership in Energy and Environmental Design) building, as rated by the nongovernmental, nonprofit U.S. Green Building Council.

Spent coffee grounds from Collections Café being used to amend soil around a hydrangea

Ladybugs being released in the garden on Earth Day

METHODS OF PRACTICED SUSTAINABILITY

WATER

When people think of Seattle, rain is one of the first images that come to mind. In the garden, we are mindful of how we can reduce our water waste. Chihuly Garden and Glass has three sections with intensive roof gardens that both delay and filter storm water and decrease the urban heat-island effect as well as carbon dioxide emissions. Intensive green roofs, having a soil depth greater than six inches, can support a more diverse collection of plants. On the green roofs at Chihuly Garden and Glass, you can find honeysuckle shrubs, floribunda roses, daylilies, Russian sage, and bearded irises, to name just a few. In addition, the vegetation grown in these gardens captures airborne pollutants, dampens noises, and creates additional wildlife habitat. Our green roofs also add to our visual aesthetic, especially considering our neighbor, the Space Needle.

The use of drip irrigation also aids in reducing water runoff, because instead of broadcasting water through sprinkler heads, we are applying it directly at the soil line at a rate that the soil, and in turn the plants, can absorb entirely. Sprinkler irrigation is still utilized in the garden but not throughout. Mulching plays an essential role in containing the water captured through rain and irrigation. By applying and maintaining a thick layer of organic material, we reduce water loss through evaporation.

SOIL FERTILITY

Soil is where it all starts. If the plants are not thriving, first the medium in which they are planted is investigated. In the garden, soil amendment products are utilized that build up the soil foundation. Through local sourcing of organic and natural products, the soil is amended based on the findings from annual soil tests. Maintaining healthy, nutrient-rich soil is pivotal in the success of our plants. Spent coffee grounds are collected on-site by Collections Café. These grounds are worked into the soil around our acid-loving shrubs, such as rhododendrons, hydrangeas, yews, and camellias. Not only do the plants benefit from the subtle drop in pH, but it diverts this organic material from our waste stream. The garden team brews compost tea weekly during the growing season and applies it to the woody plants. Compost tea is an aerobic water solution that has extracted the microbe population from compost, along with the nutrients.

PEST, DISEASE, AND WEED CONTROL

Instead of waiting to treat pest, disease, and weed issues as they arise, the garden team aims at prevention. One method is through encouragement of beneficial insect populations. By including plants such as columbine, creeping thyme, ajuga, sedum, borage, and nasturtium, we attract pollinators and other beneficial insects. Ladybugs are an important method of aphid control in the garden. Tens of thousands of ladybugs are released annually on Earth Day as part of our educational programming. By releasing ladybugs each year, we are able both to boost our naturally occurring population and to educate our guests and raise awareness of our sustainable gardening practices. It's an especially great way to engage our youngest visitors.

In alignment with our LEED certification, we aim to minimize our use of any nonorganic, unnatural, environmentally unfriendly treatments for any pest, disease, or weed. For this reason, we manually remove weeds instead of using chemicals.

REDUCTION OF NONRENEWABLE RESOURCES

Most tasks in the garden at Chihuly Garden and Glass are done with hand tools. Not only are they safer for our team members and art installations, they also do not require electric power or any fossil fuels. Rechargeable tools are secondary; they reduce waste associated with fossil fuels or nonrecyclable power sources such as batteries.

The aim is to recycle or reuse whatever possible. This decreases our negative impact on the environment and also is financially responsible. Plastic plant pots and trays are recycled if they cannot be washed and reused. Batteries are collected and recycled. Surplus coffee grounds are donated to surrounding green spaces such as other parts of Seattle Center, as are plants that no longer work in our garden setting. All the green material removed from the garden is composted, as is the food waste from the food and beverage department.

SOCIAL AWARENESS

Although Chihuly Garden and Glass is not centered on education, engaging with our guests is an opportunity that we seek. The garden experience excites, inspires, and sparks interest among many of the visitors. This creates a natural dialogue around the plants. While guests initially might be drawn to the color of the sea holly, it's the abundance of honeybees and bumblebees covering it that creates the memorable experience. Watching the hummingbirds feed off the Japanese mahonias in January is always pleasantly surprising. An arrangement of cut flowers from the garden can enhance the experience of a guest dining in our café and arouse interest in how our garden works. These moments have the ability to initiate conversation and raise awareness about sustainability in the garden, organic gardening practices, and thoughtful plant selections.

The garden at Chihuly Garden and Glass is a certified wildlife habitat, through the National Wildlife Federation. Being located in the urban core of the city, the green space is essential not only for humans but also for the birds and small mammals that round out our ecosystem. Throughout the year, garden tours are offered, along with other special events that promote awareness and highlight the organic and sustainable practices demonstrated in the garden. Collectively through multiple methods of social engagement, Chihuly Garden and Glass aims to be a piece of the puzzle in creating a generation of green thinkers.

Head gardener Shanna Jones deadheading daylilies on the green roof

Bee pollinating Rozanne cranesbill *(top)*; drip irrigation being installed near Prelude lily-of-the-valley shrub *(bottom)*

PLANT CHARTS

Celestial dogwood and Tiger Marlins (detail), 2012

Graceful ornamental onion   Globemaster ornamental onion

BULBS, CORMS, RHIZOMES, AND TUBERS

Allium amplectens 'Graceful'
Graceful ornamental onion

An American native, this allium is rabbit, rodent, and deer resistant. Plant these in clusters for the most aesthetically pleasing display. The combination of purple stamens with white petals gives a sparkling effect.

Plant Type:	Bulb	**Height:**	1'
Season of Interest:	Spring	**Spread:**	1'
Flower Color:	White	**USDA Hardiness Zone:**	4–8
Exposure:	Full sun	**Wildlife Attractions:**	Bees

Allium giganteum 'Globemaster'
Globemaster ornamental onion

'Globemaster' has softball-sized flower heads can span up to 8 inches in diameter. The flower structure is starburst-like and adds a dramatic flair to any sun-filled landscape. Best shown when planted in mass. Very drought tolerant.

Plant Type:	Bulb	**Height:**	3'
Season of Interest:	Spring	**Spread:**	2'
Flower Color:	Purple	**USDA Hardiness Zone:**	6–10
Exposure:	Full sun	**Wildlife Attractions:**	Bees

black garlic

tumbleweed onion, firework ornamental onion

Allium nigrum
black garlic

Allium nigrum is a showy, white flowering bulb with long-lasting blooms. Each tiny star-shaped flower is black in the center, providing nice color depth. Plant in mass in the landscape for the best effect. Outstanding cut and dried flower quality. Deer resistant. Drought tolerant.

Plant Type:	Bulb	**Height:**	1½-2'
Season of Interest:	Spring, Summer	**Spread:**	1-2'
Flower Color:	White	**USDA Hardiness Zone:**	4-9
Exposure:	Full sun	**Wildlife Attractions:**	Bees, Butterflies

Allium schubertii
tumbleweed onion, firework ornamental onion

The umbel flower heads of *Allium schubertii* look like a fireworks display. This bulb is known to naturalize and, once established, is drought tolerant. After blooming, dry seed heads can be left to retain interest in the landscape, or they can be used for floral arrangements.

Plant Type:	Bulb	**Height:**	1-2'
Season of Interest:	Spring	**Spread:**	1'
Flower Color:	Pink-purple	**USDA Hardiness Zone:**	5-8
Exposure:	Full sun, Part sun	**Wildlife Attractions:**	Butterflies

drumstick ornamental onion

Peruvian lily

Allium sphaerocephalon
drumstick ornamental onion

The oval-shaped flowers begin as green in color, maturing to a red-purple. An outstanding plant for the garden border, *Allium sphaerocephalon* adds a vertical element to the garden and naturalizes easily. Deer and drought resistant.

Plant Type:	Tuber	**Height:**	2-3'
Season of Interest:	Spring	**Spread:**	1'
Flower Color:	Red-purple	**USDA Hardiness Zone:**	4-8
Exposure:	Full sun	**Wildlife Attractions:**	Butterflies

Alstroemeria 'Inca Ice'
Peruvian lily

This vigorous bloomer will flower from June to frost. Peach and creamy yellow coloration with brown freckles. Great cut flower.

Plant Type:	Tuber	**Height:**	1-3'
Season of Interest:	Summer	**Spread:**	3'
Flower Color:	Peach	**USDA Hardiness Zone:**	6-9
Exposure:	Full sun, Part sun	**Wildlife Attractions:**	Hummingbirds

Blue Star Grecian windflower

White Splendour Grecian windflower

Anemone blanda 'Blue Star'
Blue Star Grecian windflower

This deer-tolerant plant with daisy-like purple flowers also sports attractive fern-like foliage. One of the harbingers of spring, it does very well as a woodland carpet plant; however, it is also used in rock gardens and even containers. Going dormant in summer, *Anemone blanda* naturalizes by tuberous rhizomes and is self-seeding.

Plant Type:	Tuber	**Height:**	6–8"
Season of Interest:	Spring	**Spread:**	3–6"
Flower Color:	Lavender	**USDA Hardiness Zone:**	5–8
Exposure:	Full sun, Part sun	**Wildlife Attractions:**	Bees

Anemone blanda 'White Splendour'
White Splendour Grecian windflower

'White Splendour' looks like a true daisy because of its white flowers with bright yellow centers. One of the harbingers of spring, it does very well as a woodland carpet plant; however, it is also used in rock gardens and even containers. Going dormant in summer, *Anemone blanda* naturalizes by tuberous rhizomes and is self-seeding. Deer tolerant.

Plant Type:	Tuber	**Height:**	6–8"
Season of Interest:	Spring	**Spread:**	3–6"
Flower Color:	White	**USDA Hardiness Zone:**	5–8
Exposure:	Full sun, Part sun	**Wildlife Attractions:**	Bees

poppy anemone, windflower

Jack-in-the-Pulpit, cobra lily

Anemone coronaria 'Mr. Fokker'
poppy anemone, windflower

Very low maintenance with a sought-after color, 'Mr. Fokker' is a great component for rock gardens and spring borders. Early spring bloomer. Summer dormant. Deadheading will promote new flowers, a rarity with bulbs. *Anemone coronaria* also makes long-lasting cut flowers.

Plant Type:	Tuber	**Height:**	2-3'
Season of Interest:	Spring	**Spread:**	1-2'
Flower Color:	Violet blue	**USDA Hardiness Zone:**	3-10
Exposure:	Full sun, Part sun, Part shade	**Wildlife Attractions:**	Bees

Arisaema nepenthoides
Jack-in-the-Pulpit, cobra lily

The spathe of *Arisaema nepenthoides* is more open than the other species and usually occurs in March or April. It possesses an attractive mottled pseudostem. There is a white spadix (a.k.a. "Jack") inside the spathe (or "pulpit"). After the spathe occurs, the leaves will emerge. Spreads by clumps and also by its own seeds. If successfully pollinated, the ripened seed heads will provide garden interest in early fall. Deer resistant.

Plant Type:	Tuber	**Height:**	1-3'
Season of Interest:	Fall, Winter, Spring	**Spread:**	1-2'
Flower Color:	Pink, Green, Brown	**USDA Hardiness Zone:**	5-8
Exposure:	Part sun, Part shade	**Wildlife Attractions:**	None

Jack-in-the-Pulpit, Japanese cobra lily

orange candleflower

Arisaema ringens
Jack-in-the-Pulpit, Japanese cobra lily

The flower is unique, hooded, and striped with white. The bright green leaves are large and look similar to trillium. This species, *ringens*, is one of the earliest to emerge in March. Long-lasting blooms. There is a white spadix (a.k.a. "Jack") inside the spathe (or "pulpit"). If successfully pollinated, the ripened seed heads will provide garden interest in early fall. Deer resistant.

Plant Type:	Tuber	**Height:**	1–2'
Season of Interest:	Fall, Winter, Spring	**Spread:**	1–2'
Flower Color:	Purple, Green	**USDA Hardiness Zone:**	6–9
Exposure:	Part shade	**Wildlife Attractions:**	None

Arum italicum 'Froggy Bottom'
orange candleflower

This stemless plant flowers in spring with a spadix that is hooded by a light green spathe. Attractive, glossy, arrowhead-shaped leaves emerge in late summer and can be up to a foot long. Excellent rain garden plant that will naturalize. Spring bloomer. Orange-red berries appear on the spadix in the summer, while the leaves and spathe disappear.

Plant Type:	Tuber	**Height:**	1–2'
Season of Interest:	Year-round	**Spread:**	1–2'
Flower Color:	Creamy white	**USDA Hardiness Zone:**	5–9
Exposure:	Part shade, Shade	**Wildlife Attractions:**	Birds

White Winter candleflower

Pink Diamond fool's onion

Arum italicum 'White Winter'
White Winter candleflower

This stemless plant flowers in spring with a spadix that is hooded by a light green spathe. The leaves of 'White Winter' feature pronounced silver veining and emerge in late summer or early fall. Excellent rain garden plant that will naturalize. Spring bloomer. Orange-red berries appear on the spadix in the summer, while the leaves and spathe disappear.

Plant Type:	Tuber	**Height:**	1-2'
Season of Interest:	Year-round	**Spread:**	1-2'
Flower Color:	Cream	**USDA Hardiness Zone:**	5-8
Exposure:	Part shade, Shade	**Wildlife Attractions:**	Birds

Brodiaea 'Pink Diamond'
Pink Diamond fool's onion

Bunches of tubular raspberry-colored flowers with light pink tips set atop tall stems. The foliage is grass-like. A great plant for a "sway effect." Brodiaea will naturalize if left undisturbed. It does well in both rock gardens and sunny borders. Perfect for floral arrangements.

Plant Type:	Bulb	**Height:**	1-2'
Season of Interest:	Spring	**Spread:**	1'
Flower Color:	Violet pink	**USDA Hardiness Zone:**	5-8
Exposure:	Full sun, Part sun	**Wildlife Attractions:**	Birds

Queen Fabiola fool's onion

Leichtlin's camass

Brodiaea 'Queen Fabiola'
Queen Fabiola fool's onion

'Queen Fabiola' has star-shaped blue-violet flowers. The foliage is grass-like. A great plant for a "sway effect." Brodiaea will naturalize if left undisturbed. It does well when planted in both rock gardens and sunny borders. Perfect for floral arrangements.

Plant Type:	Bulb	**Height:**	1–2'
Season of Interest:	Summer	**Spread:**	1'
Flower Color:	Blue-violet	**USDA Hardiness Zone:**	5–8
Exposure:	Full sun, Part sun	**Wildlife Attractions:**	Butterflies

Camassia leichtlinii 'Caerulea'
Leichtlin's camass

This Pacific Northwest native has strong supportive stems that possess star-shaped flowers that open from the bottom to the top. Dormant in summer. Best sites for this plant are in a rain garden or near a water source. Great cut flower. Will naturalize in optimal conditions. Deer and rodent tolerant.

Plant Type:	Bulb	**Height:**	2–4'
Season of Interest:	Spring	**Spread:**	1–2'
Flower Color:	Lavender	**USDA Hardiness Zone:**	5–9
Exposure:	Full sun, Part sun, Part shade	**Wildlife Attractions:**	Birds

glory of the snow

Blue Heron fumewort

Chionodoxa gigantea
glory of the snow

Blue, pendulous, bell-like flowers. Extremely tough and low maintenance. Naturalizes easily. Deer resistant. Longer-blooming, deeper in blue color, and slightly larger than the species. Exceptional plant for rock gardens and front borders, and especially effective as sweeping drifts.

Plant Type:	Bulb	**Height:**	under 6"
Season of Interest:	Spring	**Spread:**	6"
Flower Color:	Blue	**USDA Hardiness Zone:**	2–8
Exposure:	Full sun, Part sun, Part shade	**Wildlife Attractions:**	None

Corydalis curviflora var. *rosthornii* 'Blue Heron'
Blue Heron fumewort

True blue flowers are held on individual red stems, making an attractive color contrast. Gray-green ferny foliage. Compact and mounding habit. Fragrant.

Plant Type:	Bulb	**Height:**	9"
Season of Interest:	Spring, Fall	**Spread:**	12"
Flower Color:	Blue	**USDA Hardiness Zone:**	5–8
Exposure:	Part shade, Shade	**Wildlife Attractions:**	None

Beth Evans fumewort

Emily McKenzie crocosmia

Corydalis solida 'Beth Evans'
Beth Evans fumewort

Fern-like foliage. Tubular pink flowers that attractively fade with maturity. Compact and mounding habit. Summer dormant in warmer climates. Great for edging shade gardens or as understory plantings.

Plant Type:	Rhizome	**Height:**	6"
Season of Interest:	Spring	**Spread:**	6"
Flower Color:	Pink	**USDA Hardiness Zone:**	5-8
Exposure:	Part sun, Shade	**Wildlife Attractions:**	None

Crocosmia 'Emily McKenzie'
Emily McKenzie crocosmia

Glowing orange flowers with red markings bloom on stems that arch gracefully from late summer to fall. Easy to grow and tropical-looking, this cultivar has larger blooms than the species. Crocosmia makes a great long-lasting cut flower.

Plant Type:	Corm	**Height:**	2'
Season of Interest:	Summer, Winter	**Spread:**	1-2'
Flower Color:	Orange	**USDA Hardiness Zone:**	5-8
Exposure:	Full sun	**Wildlife Attractions:**	Hummingbirds

Little Redhead crocosmia

Lilac Beauty crocus

Crocosmia 'Little Redhead'
Little Redhead crocosmia

Petite form with yellow-throated coral red flowers that bloom on gracefully arched stems. Late summer bloomer. Easy to grow and tropical-looking. Crocosmia makes a great long-lasting cut flower.

Plant Type:	Corm	**Height:**	1–2'
Season of Interest:	Summer, Fall	**Spread:**	2'
Flower Color:	Red	**USDA Hardiness Zone:**	5–8
Exposure:	Full sun, Part sun	**Wildlife Attractions:**	Hummingbirds

Crocus 'Lilac Beauty'
Lilac Beauty crocus

One of the earliest crocuses to flower, lilac in color with pink throats. Grass-like foliage. It will naturalize by colonies. Summer dormancy makes these bulbs very drought tolerant. Deer resistant.

Plant Type:	Corm	**Height:**	4"
Season of Interest:	Spring	**Spread:**	4"
Flower Color:	Lilac	**USDA Hardiness Zone:**	4–8
Exposure:	Full sun, Part sun	**Wildlife Attractions:**	None

Tommasini's crocus

Persian cyclamen, winter-blooming cyclamen

Crocus tommassinianus
Tommasini's crocus

The color of this crocus often varies from silver-toned lavender to dark purple. Grass-like foliage. Summer dormancy makes these bulbs very drought tolerant. Tommasini's crocus, or "Tommies," is very low maintenance, easy to grow, and long-lived. It will naturalize by colonies. Deer resistant.

Plant Type:	Corm	**Height:**	4"
Season of Interest:	Spring	**Spread:**	4"
Flower Color:	Lavender, Purple	**USDA Hardiness Zone:**	4-8
Exposure:	Full sun	**Wildlife Attractions:**	Bees

Cyclamen coum 'Pewter Leaf Forms'
Persian cyclamen, winter-blooming cyclamen

Native to the Mediterranean and summer dormant, the foliage is a true silver that emerges in late fall and persists until spring. Flower color ranges from white to a variety of pinks. Drought and deer resistant. *Cyclamen coum* will naturalize and spreads by seeds that ants pick up and bury.

Plant Type:	Tuber	**Height:**	6"
Season of Interest:	Spring, Winter	**Spread:**	6"
Flower Color:	Pink, White	**USDA Hardiness Zone:**	5-8
Exposure:	Part sun, Part shade	**Wildlife Attractions:**	Bees

trout lily, dog tooth violet   snake's head fritillary

Erythronium 'Pagoda'
trout lily, dog tooth violet

A vigorous grower and tolerant of extreme weather conditions, 'Pagoda' has leaves that are slightly marbled. Flowers are light yellow and lily-like. Trout lily is capable of naturalizing in shady conditions.

Plant Type:	Corm	**Height:**	1'
Season of Interest:	Spring	**Spread:**	1'
Flower Color:	Soft yellow	**USDA Hardiness Zone:**	4–9
Exposure:	Full sun, Part sun	**Wildlife Attractions:**	Bees

Fritillaria meleagris
snake's head fritillary

Pendulous, bell-shaped blooms with deep purple or white checkerboard pattern. Grass-like leaves. Will naturalize. Great cut flowers. Deer resistant.

Plant Type:	Bulb	**Height:**	1'
Season of Interest:	Spring	**Spread:**	6"
Flower Color:	Deep purple/White	**USDA Hardiness Zone:**	3–8
Exposure:	Full sun, Part sun, Part shade	**Wildlife Attractions:**	Bees

giant snowdrop

spring starflower

Galanthus elwesii
giant snowdrop

A winter-blooming bulb that lasts 1–2 months, *Galanthus elwesii* is fragrant with gray-green leaves. Deer resistant.

Plant Type:	Bulb	**Height:**	4–6"
Season of Interest:	Winter	**Spread:**	2"
Flower Color:	White	**USDA Hardiness Zone:**	3–9
Exposure:	Full sun, Part sun	**Wildlife Attractions:**	Bees

Ipheion uniflorum
spring starflower

Native to Argentina, and summer dormant, the star-shaped flowers smell like honey and the foliage smells like onion.

Plant Type:	Bulb	**Height:**	9"
Season of Interest:	Spring	**Spread:**	3"
Flower Color:	White	**USDA Hardiness Zone:**	6–9
Exposure:	Full sun	**Wildlife Attractions:**	Bees

Pacific coast iris

German bearded iris

Iris 'Canyon Snow'
Pacific coast iris

Pure white flowers with yellow coloration at the base of each fall can form clumps up to 4 feet across. More vigorous and floriferous than most California native irises. With grass-like foliage and compact habit, Pacific coast irises are perfect for woodland gardens. Can tolerate drought. Deer resistant.

Plant Type:	Rhizome	**Height:**	1–2'
Season of Interest:	Spring	**Spread:**	2–3'
Flower Color:	White and yellow	**USDA Hardiness Zone:**	4–9
Exposure:	Part sun, Part shade	**Wildlife Attractions:**	Bees, Butterflies

Iris germanica 'Clarence'
German bearded iris

Upright, sturdy stems with vibrant bloom color for garden borders. Extremely fragrant. Great cut flowers. Drought and deer tolerant.

Plant Type:	Rhizome	**Height:**	3'
Season of Interest:	Spring	**Spread:**	1–2'
Flower Color:	White and blue	**USDA Hardiness Zone:**	4–9
Exposure:	Full sun	**Wildlife Attractions:**	Bees, Butterflies

autumn snowflake   tiger lily

Leucojum autumnalis
autumn snowflake

Dormant until its September bloom. White flowers are bell shaped and tinged with red at the base. Leaves are grass-like. Incredibly drought tolerant. Very fragrant.

Plant Type:	Bulb	**Height:**	8"
Season of Interest:	Fall	**Spread:**	2"
Flower Color:	White	**USDA Hardiness Zone:**	6-9
Exposure:	Full sun, Part sun	**Wildlife Attractions:**	Bees

Lilium lancifolium 'Splendens'
tiger lily

Glowing orange with black freckles. Very disease and virus resistant. Blossoms can be up to 5 inches in diameter. One stem can produce up to 25 large blooms. Excellent cut flower.

Plant Type:	Bulb	**Height:**	4-5'
Season of Interest:	Summer	**Spread:**	2-3'
Flower Color:	Orange	**USDA Hardiness Zone:**	5-8
Exposure:	Full sun, Part sun, Part shade	**Wildlife Attractions:**	Bees, Butterflies, Hummingbirds

regal lily   oriental-trumpet lily

Lilium regale 'Album'
regal lily

These yellow-throated, upward-facing, fragrant trumpet lilies are easy to grow and clump well. Stems are sturdy but may need staking. One stem can produce up to 25 large blooms.

Plant Type:	Bulb	**Height:**	4'
Season of Interest:	Summer	**Spread:**	1'
Flower Color:	White	**USDA Hardiness Zone:**	5–8
Exposure:	Full sun, Part sun	**Wildlife Attractions:**	Bees, Butterflies, Hummingbirds

Lilium ssp. 'Alchemy'
oriental-trumpet lily

Downward-facing, slightly recurved gold flower with rusty red blocks of color on the center of each petal. Fragrant 8-inch blossoms. Excellent cut flowers.

Plant Type:	Bulb	**Height:**	4–5'
Season of Interest:	Summer	**Spread:**	1–2'
Flower Color:	Gold and rust	**USDA Hardiness Zone:**	5–8
Exposure:	Full sun, Part sun	**Wildlife Attractions:**	Bees, Butterflies, Hummingbirds

grape hyacinth

hoop petticoat daffodil

Muscari latifolium
grape hyacinth

A bicolored, urn-shaped raceme comes up in March, displaying dark purple (fertile) flowers at the bottom and baby blue (sterile) flowers at the top. Only one leaf is produced per bulb, making for a tidy look. Drought tolerant once established, *Muscari latifolium* does well as an underplanting in the landscape.

Plant Type:	Bulb	**Height:**	4-6"
Season of Interest:	Spring	**Spread:**	2"
Flower Color:	Purple, Blue	**USDA Hardiness Zone:**	4-8
Exposure:	Full sun	**Wildlife Attractions:**	None

Narcissus bulbocodium 'Golden Bells'
hoop petticoat daffodil

'Golden Bells' is an improvement to the species in flower count and height. Weather resistant. Vigorous. One bulb can produce up to 20 flowers. The leaves are small and round, giving a tidier appearance to this variety than other, larger narcissus. Easy naturalizer. Squirrel resistant.

Plant Type:	Bulb	**Height:**	6-8"
Season of Interest:	Spring	**Spread:**	4-6"
Flower Color:	Yellow	**USDA Hardiness Zone:**	4-8
Exposure:	Full sun, Part sun	**Wildlife Attractions:**	Bees

Suzy daffodil

Thalia daffodil

Narcissus 'Suzy'
Suzy daffodil

Petite canary yellow daffodil with flared deep orange cups. Very fragrant. Adds a cheerful tone to both borders and containers. Excellent cut flower. Squirrel resistant.

Plant Type:	Bulb	**Height:**	1'
Season of Interest:	Spring	**Spread:**	6"
Flower Color:	Yellow	**USDA Hardiness Zone:**	4–8
Exposure:	Full sun, Part sun	**Wildlife Attractions:**	Bees

Narcissus 'Thalia'
Thalia daffodil

A multiheaded daffodil with 12-to-14-inch-long stems that is one of the earliest spring bloomers. Thalia is drought, deer, and squirrel resistant.

Plant Type:	Bulb	**Height:**	12–18"
Season of Interest:	Spring	**Spread:**	4–6"
Flower Color:	White	**USDA Hardiness Zone:**	4–8
Exposure:	Full sun, Part sun	**Wildlife Attractions:**	Bees

Siberian squill

pale yellow-eyed grass

Scilla siberica 'Spring Beauty'
Siberian squill

An extremely cold-hardy and true blue specimen, 'Spring Beauty' easily naturalizes by both seed and offshoots, and the flowers are very long-lasting. Plant in a front border or rock garden, beneath trees and naturalized areas, or even in lawns for the most striking effects.

Plant Type:	Bulb	Height:	6"
Season of Interest:	Spring	Spread:	6"
Flower Color:	Blue	USDA Hardiness Zone:	2-8
Exposure:	Full sun, Part sun, Part shade	Wildlife Attractions:	None

Sisyrinchium striatum
pale yellow-eyed grass

A member of the Iris family, this plant has several spikes of cup-shaped pale yellow blooms with butter yellow centers and faint purple stripes that arise in April. Naturalizes easily by seed. Flowers open only on sunny days. Perfect for a meadow or rock garden. Drought tolerant.

Plant Type:	Rhizome	Height:	3'
Season of Interest:	Spring	Spread:	1-2'
Flower Color:	Soft yellow	USDA Hardiness Zone:	7-10
Exposure:	Full sun, Part sun	Wildlife Attractions:	Bees

woodland tulip

calla lily

Tulipa sylvestris
woodland tulip

Because it is a species tulip, *sylvestris* will naturalize and return year after year. It does not need an extended cold period to bloom well; however, it is very cold hardy. Adds whimsy to the garden with its arching stems. Drought tolerant.

Plant Type:	Bulb	**Height:**	1'
Season of Interest:	Year-round	**Spread:**	6"
Flower Color:	Yellow	**USDA Hardiness Zone:**	4–9
Exposure:	Full sun	**Wildlife Attractions:**	None

Zantedeschia hybrid
calla lily

This tropical plant boasts elegantly shaped blooms with rose-colored throats and large bright green leaves. With its glowing effect, this variety is an excellent choice for nighttime "moon" gardens. Plant around water to allow calla lilies to benefit from the humidity. They also make wonderful container plants and are well known for their use as cut flowers.

Plant Type:	Bulb	**Height:**	3'
Season of Interest:	Summer	**Spread:**	3'
Flower Color:	White–pale pink	**USDA Hardiness Zone:**	7–10
Exposure:	Full sun, Part sun	**Wildlife Attractions:**	Bees, Butterflies

Hart's tongue fern

common lady fern

FERNS

Asplenium scolopendrium
Hart's tongue fern

Hart's tongue is an evergreen fern with leathery bright green fronds that are arching and strap-like. The frond edges have an attractive ripple effect and an interesting sori pattern. It is an exceptional shade and woodland garden plant. Deer resistant.

Plant Type:	Fern	**Height:**	1'
Season of Interest:	Year-round	**Spread:**	1'
Flower Color:	None	**USDA Hardiness Zone:**	5–8
Exposure:	Part shade, Shade	**Wildlife Attractions:**	None

Athyrium filix-femina
common lady fern

This winter-dormant fern features lacy, deeply cut, and lanceolate fronds. Lady fern possesses a clumping habit. The sori of lady fern are arranged in an inconspicuous manner on the undersides of each subleaflet, or pinnule. Easy to grow, provides soft-textured ground cover, and thrives in shady, moist environments. Deer resistant.

Plant Type:	Fern	**Height:**	3'
Season of Interest:	Spring, Summer, Fall	**Spread:**	2'
Flower Color:	None	**USDA Hardiness Zone:**	5–8
Exposure:	Part shade, Shade	**Wildlife Attractions:**	None

Chilean hard fern

alpine water fern

Blechnum chilense
Chilean hard fern

The Chilean hard fern is evergreen in milder climates and extremely robust. Despite its visual toughness, it does require the same growing environments that most ferns do in order to reach its full potential. Performs best when planted in shady moist conditions. The dark green, pinnate, and leathery fronds can provide cover for other woodland garden species. It adds architectural interest with its sturdy, tropical structure, while also contributing texture to the garden.

Plant Type:	Fern	**Height:**	3'
Season of Interest:	Year-round	**Spread:**	5'
Flower Color:	None	**USDA Hardiness Zone:**	5–8
Exposure:	Part shade, Shade	**Wildlife Attractions:**	None

Blechnum penna-marina 'Nana'
alpine water fern

Evergreen in milder climates with narrow, stunning coppery-red early spring color, this fern is best used as a short ground cover or in rockeries and other structures where crevices are likely to occur. As the fronds mature, the color transitions to a glossy green.

Plant Type:	Fern	**Height:**	10"
Season of Interest:	Year-round	**Spread:**	5'
Flower Color:	None	**USDA Hardiness Zone:**	7–9
Exposure:	Part sun, Part shade, Shade	**Wildlife Attractions:**	None

holly fern
Wallich's wood fern

Cyrtomium fortunei
holly fern

When planted in drifts with other woodland species, the holly fern is used at its best. It is evergreen in milder climates, and the fronds feature uniquely shaped leaflets that grow up to 2 feet long. Exceptional form (upright habit with arching stems) and texture give this fern great bedding potential. Fast growing and deer resistant.

Plant Type:	Fern	**Height:**	2'
Season of Interest:	Year-round	**Spread:**	2'
Flower Color:	None	**USDA Hardiness Zone:**	6-10
Exposure:	Part shade, Shade	**Wildlife Attractions:**	None

Dryopteris wallichiana
Wallich's wood fern

A stately, vase-shaped fern, it is abundant with attractive golden green "fiddle heads" in early spring. Hair-like brown scales on emerging fiddleheads add even more interest. Wallich's wood fern will give a prehistoric flair to any shade garden. It can be used as a structural component for a mid-range shade border as well as a stand-alone focal point. Deer resistant.

Plant Type:	Fern	**Height:**	4'
Season of Interest:	Spring, Summer, Fall	**Spread:**	3'
Flower Color:	None	**USDA Hardiness Zone:**	5-8
Exposure:	Part shade, Shade	**Wildlife Attractions:**	None

royal fern

Japanese tassel fern

Osmunda regalis
royal fern

Osmunda regalis is a clumping, tall, and lush sea green fern that possesses a vase-like shape at maturity. The leaflets of each frond resemble the leaves of a locust tree. Unique cinnamon brown pinnae occur in spring, rising above the fronds. Superb plant selection for gardens near water features and woodland gardens. Deer resistant.

Plant Type:	Fern	Height:	3-6'
Season of Interest:	Spring, Summer, Fall	Spread:	3'
Flower Color:	None	USDA Hardiness Zone:	5-8
Exposure:	Part shade, Shade	Wildlife Attractions:	None

Polystichum polyblepharum
Japanese tassel fern

Japanese tassel fern is an elegant addition to any shade garden edge or ground cover. With sturdy dark green fronds arching from a central crown and clumping habit, this fern also does well as a container filler. In milder climates, tassel fern is evergreen. Deer resistant.

Plant Type:	Fern	Height:	2'
Season of Interest:	Year-round	Spread:	2'
Flower Color:	None	USDA Hardiness Zone:	6-9
Exposure:	Part shade, Shade	Wildlife Attractions:	None

orange New Zealand sedge

gold-leaved Japanese forest grass

GRASSES

Carex testacea
orange New Zealand sedge

The striking bronze green and orange tones of this carex show best in fall, when the temperature begins to cool down. Full sun helps to intensify the orange and coppery tones. A clumping grass with arching blades, this plant does well in rain gardens, containers, and as a front border. *Carex testacea* is the hardiest of the New Zealand sedges. Deer resistant.

Plant Type:	Grass	Height:	2'
Season of Interest:	Spring, Summer, Fall	Spread:	2'
Flower Color:	None	USDA Hardiness Zone:	7–10
Exposure:	Full sun, Part sun, Part shade	Wildlife Attractions:	Birds

Hakonechloa macra 'Aureola'
gold-leaved Japanese forest grass

A waterfall of glowing lime green and yellow variegated grass that is perfect for woodland garden front borders, rain gardens, and containers. Full sun exposure is recommended only for sites that experience frequent rainfall or irrigation. Deer resistant.

Plant Type:	Grass	Height:	2'
Season of Interest:	Summer, Fall	Spread:	3'
Flower Color:	None	USDA Hardiness Zone:	5–9
Exposure:	Full sun, Part sun, Part shade	Wildlife Attractions:	Birds

lily turf   black mondo grass

Liriope spicata
lily turf

Liriope spicata is an excellent ground cover that naturalizes very well. A somewhat showy flower appears on erect spikes during the end of summer and is followed by black berries in fall. Evergreen in milder climates. This grass is effectively used as erosion control, in rain gardens, and in containers. Deer resistant.

Plant Type:	Grass	**Height:**	1'
Season of Interest:	Spring, Summer, Fall	**Spread:**	2'
Flower Color:	Light lavender	**USDA Hardiness Zone:**	4-10
Exposure:	Full sun, Part sun, Part shade	**Wildlife Attractions:**	Birds

Ophiopogon planiscapus 'Nigrescens'
black mondo grass

The intense black foliage color makes a dramatic and graphic statement when planted in mass. Black mondo grass also makes an attractive container accent and garden border edging. The nicely contrasting bell-shaped lavender blooms in July lead to dark purple berries and foliage in late summer and fall that can persist into the winter. Evergreen in milder climates. Tuft-like habit.

Plant Type:	Grass	**Height:**	1'
Season of Interest:	Year-round	**Spread:**	1'
Flower Color:	Lavender	**USDA Hardiness Zone:**	6-8
Exposure:	Full sun, Part sun, Part shade	**Wildlife Attractions:**	Birds

dwarf fountain grass

climbing flowering maple

Pennisetum alopecuroides 'Hameln'
dwarf fountain grass

Deep green, arching foliage. Clumping and compact habit. Evergreen in milder climates. Feathery silver-pink plumes appear in late summer, then turn brown and persist until early winter. Drought tolerant once established. It's most attractive when planted in mass. The plumes can be used in floral arrangements. Deer resistant.

Plant Type:	Grass	**Height:**	2'
Season of Interest:	Spring, Summer, Fall	**Spread:**	2'
Flower Color:	Light pink	**USDA Hardiness Zone:**	5-9
Exposure:	Full sun, Part sun, Part shade	**Wildlife Attractions:**	Birds

PERENNIALS

Abutilon × hybridum 'Nabob'
climbing flowering maple

Belonging to the same family as hibiscus, abutilon is a water-loving plant. Blooms from mid-spring to fall. Evergreen in tropical climates. Trifoliate leaves are attractive and resemble those of maples. Flowers are large, bell-shaped, and pendulous and are often called "Chinese Lanterns." 'Nabob' does well as a large container thriller, or as a backdrop massing. 'Nabob' is often referred to as climbing abutilon, but this plant doesn't attach itself to a trellis or other surface. Climbing refers more to its upright habit compared to that of other, bushier abutilons.

Plant Type:	Perennial	**Height:**	3-8'
Season of Interest:	Summer, Fall, Winter	**Spread:**	3-5'
Flower Color:	Dark red	**USDA Hardiness Zone:**	9-11
Exposure:	Full sun, Part sun	**Wildlife Attractions:**	Bees, Butterflies, Hummingbirds

Kentish Belle climbing abutilon

flowering maple

Abutilon megapotamicum 'Kentish Belle'
Kentish Belle climbing abutilon

One of the hardiest of the species, *megapotamicum* is also one of the longest-blooming and can easily be trained onto a wall or fence. It also plays a great role as a specimen or patio plant. Its flowers are slightly funnel-shaped, soft orange with a dark red calyx, and pendulous. Easy to grow, it can reach considerable height, while still maintaining a loose vase shape. 'Kentish Belle' is often referred to as climbing abutilon, but this plant doesn't attach itself to a trellis or other surface. Climbing refers more to its upright habit compared to that of other, bushier abutilons.

Plant Type:	Perennial	**Height:**	5'
Season of Interest:	Summer, Fall	**Spread:**	5'
Flower Color:	Orange and red	**USDA Hardiness Zone:**	5-8
Exposure:	Full sun, Part sun	**Wildlife Attractions:**	Bees, Butterflies, Hummingbirds

Abutilon 'Tiger Eye'
flowering maple

This fast-growing ornamental maple has striking bell-shaped flowers that appear in late spring and continue to bloom until the first frost. Able to control size and habit with a hard yearly cutback.

Plant Type:	Perennial	**Height:**	5-8'
Season of Interest:	Summer, Fall	**Spread:**	3-4'
Flower Color:	Yellow with red veining	**USDA Hardiness Zone:**	9-11
Exposure:	Full sun, Part sun	**Wildlife Attractions:**	Bees

purple sheep's burr

New Zealand burr

Acaena inermis 'Purpurea'
purple sheep's burr

Extremely low-maintenance evergreen ground cover. Foliage is a deep purple-burgundy color.

Plant Type:	Perennial	**Height:**	<6"
Season of Interest:	Year-round	**Spread:**	1-3'
Flower Color:	Brown	**USDA Hardiness Zone:**	6-9
Exposure:	Full sun	**Wildlife Attractions:**	None

Acaena saccaticupula 'Blue Haze'
New Zealand burr

Similar to 'Purpurea', but foliage has a lovely, soft blue-green color.

Plant Type:	Perennial	**Height:**	<6"
Season of Interest:	Year-round	**Spread:**	1-3'
Flower Color:	Brown	**USDA Hardiness Zone:**	6-9
Exposure:	Full sun	**Wildlife Attractions:**	None

dwarf bear's breeches

hummingbird mint

Acanthus spinosus
dwarf bear's breeches

This is a clump-forming perennial that can be quite showy with its gorgeous foliage and tall flower spikes reaching up to 24 inches. Deer resistant. The compact habit makes it easy to fit into any garden. Spiny foliage and flower stalks make this useful as a barrier planting.

Plant Type:	Perennial	Height:	2'
Season of Interest:	Spring, Summer	Spread:	2'
Flower Color:	Light purple, Pink, White	USDA Hardiness Zone:	5-9
Exposure:	Full sun, Part sun	Wildlife Attractions:	Bees

Agastache 'Blue Boa'
hummingbird mint

Long-blooming and scented purple flowers attract pollinators! Heat and humidity tolerance adds to the value of this plant.

Plant Type:	Perennial	Height:	2'
Season of Interest:	Summer	Spread:	2'
Flower Color:	Purple	USDA Hardiness Zone:	5-10
Exposure:	Full sun	Wildlife Attractions:	Bees, Butterflies, Hummingbirds

mouse plant   dwarf goat's beard

Arisarum proboscideum
mouse plant

Best grown in shady woodland gardens. Place in an area where the hidden flowers can be enjoyed close up.

Plant Type:	Perennial	**Height:**	<6"
Season of Interest:	Spring	**Spread:**	<6"
Flower Color:	Maroon	**USDA Hardiness Zone:**	7-9
Exposure:	Part shade, Shade	**Wildlife Attractions:**	None

Aruncus aethusifolius
dwarf goat's beard

Dwarf variety of goat's beard has finely cut foliage that has a fern-like appearance. Most effective when planted in mass.

Plant Type:	Perennial	**Height:**	12"
Season of Interest:	Spring	**Spread:**	18"
Flower Color:	Ivory	**USDA Hardiness Zone:**	3-9
Exposure:	Part shade, Shade	**Wildlife Attractions:**	None

goat's beard

Chinese wild ginger

Aruncus dioicus
goat's beard

Goat's beard has light and airy foliage and flower plumes that make it a nice backdrop planting in the landscape. On a breezy day, it adds movement in the garden. This is a great plant for water and woodland gardens. Deer resistant.

Plant Type:	Perennial	**Height:**	4–6'
Season of Interest:	Spring	**Spread:**	4–6'
Flower Color:	Ivory	**USDA Hardiness Zone:**	4–8
Exposure:	Part shade, Shade	**Wildlife Attractions:**	None

Asarum splendens
Chinese wild ginger

The silver and blue-green patterned foliage is arrow-shaped. Very curious, cup-shaped flowers are hidden beneath. Plant in an area where the blooms can be enjoyed close up. Deer resistant.

Plant Type:	Perennial	**Height:**	12"
Season of Interest:	Spring	**Spread:**	9"
Flower Color:	Purple-brown	**USDA Hardiness Zone:**	7–9
Exposure:	Part shade, Shade	**Wildlife Attractions:**	None

wood aster

Prince calico aster

Aster cordifolius 'Avondale'
wood aster

Excellent choice for an early fall bloomer for either shade or sun. Attractively used as a mass planting and as woodland edging. Drought tolerant once established and deer resistant.

Plant Type:	Perennial	**Height:**	3'
Season of Interest:	Fall	**Spread:**	2'
Flower Color:	Blue-lavender	**USDA Hardiness Zone:**	4-9
Exposure:	Full sun	**Wildlife Attractions:**	Butterflies

Aster lateriflorus 'Prince'
Prince calico aster

The deep-maroon-colored foliage of 'Prince' combined with the finely textured blooms creates a beautiful contrast for fall gardens. Very floriferous and tolerant of a wide range of soil conditions.

Plant Type:	Perennial	**Height:**	3'
Season of Interest:	Fall	**Spread:**	3'
Flower Color:	Purple/White	**USDA Hardiness Zone:**	5-9
Exposure:	Full sun	**Wildlife Attractions:**	Bees, Butterflies

astilboides

beesia

Astilboides tabularis (a.k.a. *Rodgersia tabularis*)
astilboides

The leaves of astilboides are peltate, large, lobed, and impressively showy. The flower is similar to that of astilbes but with a much taller flower stalk. Keep soil moist during the growing season to avoid leaf burn.

Plant Type:	Perennial	**Height:**	3-4'
Season of Interest:	Spring, Summer	**Spread:**	2-3'
Flower Color:	White	**USDA Hardiness Zone:**	5-7
Exposure:	Part shade, Shade	**Wildlife Attractions:**	None

Beesia calthifolia
beesia

Beesia is a lush and attractive evergreen ground cover in a woodland or shade garden setting. It sends up tall spikes of tiny white flowers in the spring. Prefers well-drained soil. A native to China with leathery, heart-shaped leaves; its discovery has an interesting history.

Plant Type:	Perennial	**Height:**	12"
Season of Interest:	Year-round	**Spread:**	18"
Flower Color:	White	**USDA Hardiness Zone:**	6-9
Exposure:	Part shade, Shade	**Wildlife Attractions:**	Bees

beesia

double cuckoo flower

Beesia deltophylla
beesia

Beesia is a lush and attractive evergreen ground cover in a woodland or shade setting. It sends up tall spikes of tiny white flowers in the spring. *Beesia deltophylla* has roughly 15 "teeth" on each side of its leaves, differentiating it from *Beesia calthifolia*, which has a total of around 50.

Plant Type:	Perennial	**Height:**	12"
Season of Interest:	Year-round	**Spread:**	18"
Flower Color:	White	**USDA Hardiness Zone:**	6-9
Exposure:	Part shade, Shade	**Wildlife Attractions:**	Bees

Cardamine pratensis 'Flore-pleno'
double cuckoo flower

The double cuckoo flower likes to grow near water or as an understory planting. Spreads slowly. Edible and in the same family as cabbage and broccoli.

Plant Type:	Perennial	**Height:**	10"
Season of Interest:	Spring, Summer	**Spread:**	12"
Flower Color:	Pale pink-white	**USDA Hardiness Zone:**	5-9
Exposure:	Part sun, Part shade	**Wildlife Attractions:**	Butterflies

Dixter Orange chrysanthemum   meadow orchid

Chrysanthemum 'Dixter Orange'
Dixter Orange chrysanthemum

Masses of double pom-pom-shaped blooms appear in September here. With a clumping habit and strong stems, there is no need to stake this plant. Insert into garden borders and use in fall containers.

Plant Type:	Perennial	Height:	3'
Season of Interest:	Fall	Spread:	2'
Flower Color:	Burnt orange	USDA Hardiness Zone:	5–9
Exposure:	Full sun, Part sun	Wildlife Attractions:	Bees

Dactylorhiza fuchsii 'Bressingham Bonus'
meadow orchid

A terrestrial orchid, it naturalizes well. Meadow orchid is a perfect plant choice for part-shade woodland gardens. True violet in color.

Plant Type:	Perennial	Height:	18"
Season of Interest:	Spring	Spread:	10"
Flower Color:	Violet	USDA Hardiness Zone:	5–9
Exposure:	Part sun, Part shade	Wildlife Attractions:	None

Green Jewel coneflower

Amber Queen barrenwort

Echinacea 'Green Jewel'
Green Jewel coneflower

Green Jewel has a longer-than-average bloom time here, beginning in May and ending in mid-October. Light green petals surround dark green center cones on this Echinacea. With its unique color and sturdy stems, this variety makes a wonderful cut flower and looks best when planted in groups and paired with purple and blue tones.

Plant Type:	Perennial	**Height:**	1½–2'
Season of Interest:	Spring, Summer, Fall	**Spread:**	1–1½'
Flower Color:	Light green	**USDA Hardiness Zone:**	3–8
Exposure:	Full sun, Part sun	**Wildlife Attractions:**	Birds, Butterflies

Epimedium 'Amber Queen'
Amber Queen barrenwort

Amber Queen barrenwort's new foliage is heavily flecked in maroon. Its spidery, 1-inch amber yellow flowers are tipped in orange-red. In April, it presents its peak bloom, but repeat flowering occurs until midsummer. Deer resistant, semi-evergreen with spiny green leaves.

Plant Type:	Perennial	**Height:**	2'
Season of Interest:	Spring, Summer	**Spread:**	3'
Flower Color:	Yellow	**USDA Hardiness Zone:**	5–8
Exposure:	Part sun, Part shade	**Wildlife Attractions:**	None

Domino barrenwort

Lilafee barrenwort

Epimedium 'Domino'
Domino barrenwort

The leaves of Domino barrenwort are spiny and green flecked with amber. Large white spurred flowers are arching and tipped with maroon. Deer resistant and very floriferous.

Plant Type:	Perennial	Height:	2'
Season of Interest:	Spring	Spread:	3'
Flower Color:	White	USDA Hardiness Zone:	5–8
Exposure:	Part sun, Part shade	Wildlife Attractions:	Bees

Epimedium grandiflorum 'Lilafee'
Lilafee barrenwort

Ten-inch-tall flower spikes are adorned with violet blooms. Can tolerate drought and dry shade. Deciduous foliage is a lavender bronze when emerging in early spring. 'Lilafee' is synonymous with 'Lilac Fairy'.

Plant Type:	Perennial	Height:	12"
Season of Interest:	Spring	Spread:	10–13"
Flower Color:	Violet	USDA Hardiness Zone:	5–8
Exposure:	Part sun, Part shade	Wildlife Attractions:	None

Cherry Tart barrenwort

Sapphire Blue sea holly

Epimedium × versicolor 'Cherry Tart'
Cherry Tart barrenwort

Rose pink sepals with cherry-red spurs. Reddish-purple foliage appears in spring. Deer resistant.

Plant Type:	Perennial	**Height:**	12–15"
Season of Interest:	Spring	**Spread:**	12"
Flower Color:	Pink	**USDA Hardiness Zone:**	5–8
Exposure:	Part sun, Part shade	**Wildlife Attractions:**	None

Eryngium 'Sapphire Blue'
Sapphire Blue sea holly

Intense steel blue stems, upper leaves, and flowers. Sturdy, upright habit. This Mediterranean native is drought, salt, and poor soil tolerant. Works great as long-lasting floral arrangement components.

Plant Type:	Perennial	**Height:**	24–30"
Season of Interest:	Spring, Summer	**Spread:**	18–24"
Flower Color:	Blue	**USDA Hardiness Zone:**	4–9
Exposure:	Full sun	**Wildlife Attractions:**	Bees

Aurea fuchsia

white hardy fuchsia

Fuchsia magellanica 'Aurea'
Aurea fuchsia

Chartreuse foliage is striking in a shady area of the garden. The magenta and purple, bell-shaped flowers add to the show, starting in early summer and continuing into the fall.

Plant Type:	Perennial	**Height:**	2-3'
Season of Interest:	Summer, Fall	**Spread:**	2-3'
Flower Color:	Magenta with purple	**USDA Hardiness Zone:**	6-8
Exposure:	Full sun, Part sun, Part shade, Shade	**Wildlife Attractions:**	Bees, Hummingbirds

Fuchsia magellanica 'Hawkshead'
white hardy fuchsia

This hardy fuchsia has white, bell-shaped flowers early summer through the fall.

Plant Type:	Perennial	**Height:**	3'
Season of Interest:	Summer, Fall	**Spread:**	3'
Flower Color:	White	**USDA Hardiness Zone:**	7-9
Exposure:	Full sun, Part sun, Part shade	**Wildlife Attractions:**	Bees, Hummingbirds

Mrs. Popple fuchsia

trumpet gentian

Fuchsia 'Mrs. Popple'
Mrs. Popple fuchsia

Showy, bell-shaped flowers bloom early summer through the fall.

Plant Type:	Perennial	**Height:**	4–6'
Season of Interest:	Summer, Fall	**Spread:**	4–6'
Flower Color:	Magenta with purple	**USDA Hardiness Zone:**	8–10
Exposure:	Full sun, Part sun, Part shade	**Wildlife Attractions:**	Bees, Hummingbirds

Gentiana acaulis 'Maxima'
trumpet gentian

A true blue color! These trumpet-shaped flowers bloom in early spring. Alpine native performs best in well-drained soil.

Plant Type:	Perennial	**Height:**	1'
Season of Interest:	Spring	**Spread:**	1–3'
Flower Color:	Royal blue	**USDA Hardiness Zone:**	4–8
Exposure:	Part sun, Part shade	**Wildlife Attractions:**	None

St. Ola cranesbill

Rozanne cranesbill

Geranium × *cantabrigiense* 'St. Ola'
St. Ola cranesbill

This hardy geranium stays tight to the ground, making it a nice ground cover with soft pink/white blooms in spring.

Plant Type:	Perennial	**Height:**	1'
Season of Interest:	Spring	**Spread:**	2'
Flower Color:	Soft pink/White	**USDA Hardiness Zone:**	4–8
Exposure:	Full sun, Part sun, Part shade	**Wildlife Attractions:**	Bees, Butterflies

Geranium 'Rozanne'
Rozanne cranesbill

A workhorse in the garden. 'Rozanne' blooms steadily from late spring to the first frost. Plant forms soft mounds.

Plant Type:	Perennial	**Height:**	2–3'
Season of Interest:	Summer	**Spread:**	2–3'
Flower Color:	Purple	**USDA Hardiness Zone:**	4–8
Exposure:	Full sun, Part sun, Part shade	**Wildlife Attractions:**	Bees, Butterflies

Totally Tangerine geum

Cinnamon Snow Lenten rose

Geum 'Totally Tangerine'
Totally Tangerine geum

Light, airy clusters of vibrant orange flowers in mid-spring. Deadhead to encourage an encore show of blooms.

Plant Type:	Perennial	Height:	2–3'
Season of Interest:	Spring, Summer	Spread:	2'
Flower Color:	Orange	USDA Hardiness Zone:	4–8
Exposure:	Full sun, Part sun	Wildlife Attractions:	Bees

Helleborus × ballardiae 'Cinnamon Snow'
Cinnamon Snow Lenten rose

Winter-blooming perennial flowers when the rest of the garden is still asleep. Long-lasting blooms. Deer resistant.

Plant Type:	Perennial	Height:	18"
Season of Interest:	Winter, Spring	Spread:	24"
Flower Color:	Cream with rose and cinnamon tones	USDA Hardiness Zone:	5–9
Exposure:	Part shade, Shade	Wildlife Attractions:	None

Pink Frost Lenten rose

Silver Moon Lenten rose

Helleborus × *ballardiae* 'Pink Frost'
Pink Frost Lenten rose

The burgundy stems of these Lenten roses hold up long-lasting flowers that are a variety of pink tones. Deer resistant.

Plant Type:	Perennial	**Height:**	18"
Season of Interest:	Winter, Spring	**Spread:**	24"
Flower Color:	Pink	**USDA Hardiness Zone:**	5-9
Exposure:	Part shade, Shade	**Wildlife Attractions:**	None

Helleborus × *ericsmithii* 'Silver Moon'
Silver Moon Lenten rose

Silvery foliage sets this variety apart from other Lenten roses. Deer resistant.

Plant Type:	Perennial	**Height:**	2'
Season of Interest:	Spring	**Spread:**	1-2'
Flower Color:	White with pink tones	**USDA Hardiness Zone:**	5-8
Exposure:	Part shade, Shade	**Wildlife Attractions:**	None

Black Diamond Lenten rose

White Pearl Lenten rose

Helleborus × hybridus 'Black Diamond'
Black Diamond Lenten rose

Unique black flowers help this stand apart from other hellebore varieties. Long-lasting blooms. Deer resistant.

Plant Type:	Perennial	**Height:**	18"
Season of Interest:	Winter, Spring	**Spread:**	24"
Flower Color:	Deep purple/Black	**USDA Hardiness Zone:**	5-9
Exposure:	Part shade, Shade	**Wildlife Attractions:**	None

Helleborus × hybridus 'White Pearl'
White Pearl Lenten rose

A showy perennial that provides outstanding winter interest. Great as a cut flower. Deer resistant.

Plant Type:	Perennial	**Height:**	12"
Season of Interest:	Winter, Spring	**Spread:**	24"
Flower Color:	White with burgundy centers	**USDA Hardiness Zone:**	4-8
Exposure:	Part shade, Shade	**Wildlife Attractions:**	None

Josef Lemper Christmas rose

scarlet daylily

Helleborus niger 'Josef Lemper'
Josef Lemper Christmas rose

An earlier bloomer than other hellebore varieties. Deer resistant.

Plant Type:	Perennial	**Height:**	12"
Season of Interest:	Winter	**Spread:**	18"
Flower Color:	White	**USDA Hardiness Zone:**	4–8
Exposure:	Part shade, Shade	**Wildlife Attractions:**	None

Hemerocallis 'Breathless Beauty'
scarlet daylily

Scarlet blooms appear in midsummer on long flower stems. Deadhead to maintain cleanliness and lengthen bloom period.

Plant Type:	Perennial	**Height:**	3'
Season of Interest:	Summer	**Spread:**	3'
Flower Color:	Scarlet	**USDA Hardiness Zone:**	3–9
Exposure:	Full sun, Part sun	**Wildlife Attractions:**	Bees, Butterflies, Hummingbirds

Obsidian coral bells

Plum Pudding coral bells

Heuchera 'Obsidian'
Obsidian coral bells

Burgundy foliage adds contrast to the garden. Performs best in part sun/shade in well-drained soil.

Plant Type:	Perennial	**Height:**	24"
Season of Interest:	Spring, Summer	**Spread:**	24"
Flower Color:	Cream	**USDA Hardiness Zone:**	4-9
Exposure:	Part sun, Part shade	**Wildlife Attractions:**	Bees, Butterflies

Heuchera 'Plum Pudding'
Plum Pudding coral bells

'Plum Pudding' has mounding and semi-evergreen purple foliage with a silver veneer and white sprays of flowers in spring. Will need more regular waterings if grown in full sun. Appreciates well-drained soil.

Plant Type:	Perennial	**Height:**	24"
Season of Interest:	Spring, Summer	**Spread:**	24"
Flower Color:	White	**USDA Hardiness Zone:**	4-9
Exposure:	Part sun, Part shade	**Wildlife Attractions:**	Bees, Butterflies

English lavender

pachyphragma

Lavandula angustifolia 'Hidcote'
English lavender

This traditional English lavender has a beautiful fragrance. Soft lavender blooms appear in late spring to early summer. Deadhead to encourage prolonged bloom period. Edible culinary herb.

Plant Type:	Perennial	**Height:**	18"
Season of Interest:	Spring, Summer	**Spread:**	18"
Flower Color:	Lavender	**USDA Hardiness Zone:**	5–8
Exposure:	Part sun, Part shade	**Wildlife Attractions:**	Bees, Butterflies

Pachyphragma macrophyllum
pachyphragma

Mounds of heart-shaped leaves sit below clusters of white flowers in spring. Heat tolerant. Great used as an underplanting.

Plant Type:	Perennial	**Height:**	1–3'
Season of Interest:	Spring	**Spread:**	1–3'
Flower Color:	White	**USDA Hardiness Zone:**	5–9
Exposure:	Full sun, Part sun, Part shade	**Wildlife Attractions:**	None

Lacey Blue Russian sage

Sundowner New Zealand flax

Perovskia atriplicifolia
Lacey Blue Russian sage

Drought tolerant once established. Deer resistant. A cooler tone for the landscape, boasting silver-green foliage and lavender blue blooms. Upright habit. Cut back in winter for fresh blooms in spring.

Plant Type:	Perennial	Height:	4'
Season of Interest:	Summer, Fall	Spread:	3'
Flower Color:	Lavender	USDA Hardiness Zone:	5–9
Exposure:	Full sun	Wildlife Attractions:	Bees, Butterflies

Phormium 'Sundowner'
Sundowner New Zealand flax

Multi-tonal arching leaf blades add a tropical feel in the garden. Evergreen leaves can be used in floral arrangements.

Plant Type:	Perennial	Height:	5'
Season of Interest:	Year-round	Spread:	4–6'
Flower Color:	Insignificant	USDA Hardiness Zone:	8–11
Exposure:	Full sun	Wildlife Attractions:	None

Dusky Chief New Zealand flax

cape fuchsia

Phormium tenax 'Dusky Chief'
Dusky Chief New Zealand flax

Deep burgundy, strap-like leaves give this *Phormium* a tropical appeal in the landscape. Great backdrop planting or as a single specimen.

Plant Type:	Perennial	**Height:**	4–8'
Season of Interest:	Year-round	**Spread:**	4–6'
Flower Color:	Insignificant	**USDA Hardiness Zone:**	8–11
Exposure:	Full sun	**Wildlife Attractions:**	None

Phygelius aequalis 'Moonraker'
cape fuchsia

This South Africa native has soft yellow, tubular flowers. The plant spreads by runners.

Plant Type:	Perennial	**Height:**	3–4'
Season of Interest:	Summer	**Spread:**	2'
Flower Color:	Soft yellow	**USDA Hardiness Zone:**	7–9
Exposure:	Full sun, Part sun, Part shade	**Wildlife Attractions:**	Bees, Hummingbirds

giant mayapple

primrose

Podophyllum pleianthum
giant mayapple

Leaves emerge from the ground in early spring like glossy green mushrooms and then open like umbrellas to resemble lily pads. Clusters of burgundy, bell-shaped flowers hang hidden below each leaf, followed by showy fruit. Prefers moist soil and may self-seed. This plant is a great addition to any shade garden!

Plant Type:	Perennial	**Height:**	24"
Season of Interest:	Spring	**Spread:**	18"
Flower Color:	Burgundy	**USDA Hardiness Zone:**	6–8
Exposure:	Part shade, Shade	**Wildlife Attractions:**	None

Primula (Barnhaven Collection)

includes: *Primula* 'Chartreuse', *Primula* 'Desert Sunset', *Primula* 'Gilded Ginger', *Primula* 'Harbour Lights', *Primula* × *juliana* 'Jay Jay', *Primula* 'Little Egypt', *Primula* 'Midnight', *Primula* 'Paris 90', *Primula* 'Sorbet', *Primula* 'Spice Shades'

This primrose collection adds much-needed color in the late winter to the early spring seasons. Most effective when massed together; the old-world colors are striking. From coppery rust tones to soft yellows and deep violets, these primroses have stood the test of time. Seaweed fertilizer helps to boost the bloom size and duration.

Plant Type:	Perennial	**Height:**	12"
Season of Interest:	Winter, Spring	**Spread:**	12"
Flower Color:	Varies	**USDA Hardiness Zone:**	5–8
Exposure:	Part sun, Part shade	**Wildlife Attractions:**	Bees

Late Snow Japanese primrose

Pastel Pink Japanese primrose

Primula sieboldii 'Late Snow'
Late Snow Japanese primrose

The delicately cut petals of 'Late Snow' resemble snowflakes in early spring.

Plant Type:	Perennial	**Height:**	12"
Season of Interest:	Spring	**Spread:**	12"
Flower Color:	White	**USDA Hardiness Zone:**	5-8
Exposure:	Part sun, Part shade	**Wildlife Attractions:**	Bees

Primula sieboldii 'Pastel Pink'
Pastel Pink Japanese primrose

Similar to 'Late Snow' but with a soft pink-lavender bloom.

Plant Type:	Perennial	**Height:**	12"
Season of Interest:	Spring	**Spread:**	12"
Flower Color:	Pale pink-lavender	**USDA Hardiness Zone:**	5-8
Exposure:	Part sun, Part shade	**Wildlife Attractions:**	Bees

lesser celandine   red-veined dock, bloody dock

Ranunculus ficaria 'Solomon's White'
lesser celandine

A rock garden plant that initially appears in mid-February and blooms with daisy-like white flowers in mid-March here, 'Solomon's White' is also deer resistant. The flowers boast bright yellow centers, and the leaves are glossy and heart-shaped. This ranunculus is totally dormant by late May.

Plant Type:	Perennial	**Height:**	3"
Season of Interest:	Spring	**Spread:**	6"
Flower Color:	White with yellow center	**USDA Hardiness Zone:**	4–9
Exposure:	Part sun, Part shade	**Wildlife Attractions:**	Bees

Rumex sanguineus
red-veined dock, bloody dock

Grown primarily for its foliage, *Rumex* is a rosette-shaped, clumping plant that produces green leaves marked with dark red and purple veins. Wonderful to use in containers and in front borders. We remove the flowers to discourage self-seeding and to promote leaf growth.

Plant Type:	Perennial	**Height:**	1'
Season of Interest:	Spring, Summer, Fall	**Spread:**	2'
Flower Color:	None	**USDA Hardiness Zone:**	5–8
Exposure:	Full sun, Part sun, Part shade	**Wildlife Attractions:**	None

Red Velvet Texas sage

cotton lavender

Salvia greggii 'Red Velvet'
Red Velvet Texas sage

Crimson red, large flowers adorn this salvia. A long-blooming plant, 'Red Velvet' performs best in the late summer and fall here. Bright green foliage. Drought, heat, and deer resistant.

Plant Type:	Perennial	**Height:**	3'
Season of Interest:	Spring, Summer, Fall	**Spread:**	3'
Flower Color:	Red	**USDA Hardiness Zone:**	7–10
Exposure:	Full sun, Part sun	**Wildlife Attractions:**	Bees, Butterflies, Hummingbirds

Santolina chamaecyparissus 'Pretty Carroll'
cotton lavender

A small Mediterranean shrub with aromatic, evergreen foliage and flowers. Small pom-pom-shaped blooms adorn its rounded habit in the summer. Foliage adds both texture and a cool silver tone to the garden. Best used as a front bed border or a container component.

Plant Type:	Perennial	**Height:**	12–18"
Season of Interest:	Summer	**Spread:**	24"
Flower Color:	Yellow	**USDA Hardiness Zone:**	6–9
Exposure:	Full sun	**Wildlife Attractions:**	Bees

toothed saxifrage

Aureum sedum

Saxifraga × geum 'Dentata'
toothed saxifrage

The leaves of 'Dentata' are small, round, leathery, and toothed. Delicate, star-shaped white flowers appear in the spring on maroon stems. Evergreen. Excellent ground cover or rock garden specimen.

Plant Type:	Perennial	**Height:**	8"
Season of Interest:	Year-round	**Spread:**	1'
Flower Color:	White	**USDA Hardiness Zone:**	6–9
Exposure:	Full sun, Part sun, Part shade	**Wildlife Attractions:**	Butterflies

Sedum acre 'Aureum'
Aureum sedum

An evergreen ground cover, 'Aureum' is a relatively fast grower that thrives in full sun and poor-quality soils. Easy to grow and care for, the new growth is a chartreuse color, and very small yellow, star-shaped flowers emerge in early summer. The texture of this sedum is an added bonus to the garden, but it also works well in containers. Rabbit and deer resistant.

Plant Type:	Perennial	**Height:**	12"
Season of Interest:	Spring, Summer	**Spread:**	20"
Flower Color:	Yellow	**USDA Hardiness Zone:**	4–9
Exposure:	Full sun	**Wildlife Attractions:**	Butterflies

Angelina sedum

Turquoise Tails sedum

Sedum rupestre 'Angelina'
Angelina sedum

An evergreen stonecrop that possesses a needle-like texture, 'Angelina' is a great choice for the landscape as a ground cover. It is also an excellent spiller or filler plant for hanging baskets and containers. Colder fall and winter temps result in orange coloration of foliage. Yellow blooms appear from June to August. Drought, heat, and deer tolerant.

Plant Type:	Perennial	**Height:**	6"
Season of Interest:	Summer, Fall, Winter	**Spread:**	24"
Flower Color:	Yellow	**USDA Hardiness Zone:**	4–9
Exposure:	Full sun, Part sun	**Wildlife Attractions:**	Bees

Sedum sediforme 'Turquoise Tails'
Turquoise Tails sedum

'Turquoise Tails' is a gray-blue sedum with needle-like foliage that is evergreen. Blooms in June and July. These plants make great accents or container components. Group in masses for landscapes. Drought, heat, and deer tolerant.

Plant Type:	Perennial	**Height:**	6"
Season of Interest:	Summer	**Spread:**	12"
Flower Color:	Creamy yellow	**USDA Hardiness Zone:**	5–10
Exposure:	Full sun, Part sun	**Wildlife Attractions:**	Bees

Cobweb Buttons Hen and Chicks

Royal Ruby Hen and Chicks

Sempervivum arachnoideum 'Cobweb Buttons'
Cobweb Buttons Hen and Chicks

The gray-green and red foliage color is brightened by a white webbing. Very showy, compact, and easy to grow. Evergreen. Resistant to aphids, slugs, and snails. Drought tolerant and does not require fertilization. Appreciates adequate drainage.

Plant Type:	Perennial	**Height:**	4"
Season of Interest:	Year-round	**Spread:**	12"
Flower Color:	Pink	**USDA Hardiness Zone:**	4-9
Exposure:	Full sun	**Wildlife Attractions:**	None

Sempervivum tectorum 'Royal Ruby'
Royal Ruby Hen and Chicks

Clumping rosettes of red fleshy leaves produce several offspring of miniature rosettes that surround the main plant, hence the common name, "Hen and Chicks." Easy to care for (and simple to propagate), 'Royal Ruby' is a beautiful coppery red in color. Fast growing and drought tolerant. Excellent ground cover and container plant. Evergreen.

Plant Type:	Perennial	**Height:**	4-8"
Season of Interest:	Year-round	**Spread:**	12"
Flower Color:	Light pink	**USDA Hardiness Zone:**	4-9
Exposure:	Full sun	**Wildlife Attractions:**	None

Sunset Hen and Chicks   Miyazaki toad lily

Sempervivum tectorum 'Sunset'
Sunset Hen and Chicks

'Sunset' is lime green with maroon- and orange-tipped succulent leaves. With cooler temperatures, the leaves turn burgundy and bronze.

Plant Type:	Perennial	**Height:**	2–4"
Season of Interest:	Year-round	**Spread:**	6–8"
Flower Color:	Light pink	**USDA Hardiness Zone:**	4–9
Exposure:	Full sun	**Wildlife Attractions:**	None

Tricyrtis hirta 'Miyazaki'
Miyazaki toad lily

'Miyazaki' has a shorter, more arching habit than the original species. Spotted with purple and white, the orchid-like flowers emerge from the leaf axils in late summer and early fall. Green foliage has deep purple mottling. *Tricyrtis* is the perfect plant for dry shade. As it is not rhizomatous, 'Miyazaki' is tightly clumping and does not spread as well as some of the other species.

Plant Type:	Perennial	**Height:**	24"
Season of Interest:	Summer, Fall	**Spread:**	18"
Flower Color:	Purple and white	**USDA Hardiness Zone:**	4–8
Exposure:	Part shade, Shade	**Wildlife Attractions:**	None

purple top verbena

Rozannie aucuba

Verbena bonariensis
purple top verbena

This verbena gives structure, texture, and color to garden borders. The stems are willowy but sturdy; they do not require staking. Great as a backdrop planting in an annual or perennial bed. Adds movement to the garden on a breezy day. Long blooming and drought tolerant, purple top verbena will naturalize even if it doesn't overwinter.

Plant Type:	Perennial	**Height:**	3-6'
Season of Interest:	Summer	**Spread:**	1-3'
Flower Color:	Violet	**USDA Hardiness Zone:**	7-11
Exposure:	Full sun, Part sun	**Wildlife Attractions:**	Birds, Butterflies

SHRUBS

Aucuba japonica 'Rozannie'
Rozannie aucuba

A glossy-leaved, evergreen shrub that possesses a compact habit. Salt tolerant. Attractive red berries occur in late summer and fall. 'Rozannie' works well as a low-hedging or back-border plant for dry shade areas. Deer tolerant. Drought tolerant once established.

Plant Type:	Shrub	**Height:**	4'
Season of Interest:	Year-round	**Spread:**	4'
Flower Color:	Purple	**USDA Hardiness Zone:**	6-9
Exposure:	Shade	**Wildlife Attractions:**	None

William Penn barberry   Profusion beautyberry

Berberis × *gladwynnensis* 'William Penn'
William Penn barberry

The glossy dark green foliage of this barberry turns to an attractive bronze in the fall. Yellow flowers occur in the spring. Purple berries are developed after flower and remain until September. Its evergreen quality gives 'William Penn' interest for winter and beyond. It is a fast grower. Deer resistant. The half-inch spines on the branches make this a great plant for a defensive screening hedge.

Plant Type:	Shrub	**Height:**	4'
Season of Interest:	Year-round	**Spread:**	5'
Flower Color:	Yellow	**USDA Hardiness Zone:**	5-8
Exposure:	Full sun, Part sun	**Wildlife Attractions:**	Birds

Callicarpa 'Profusion'
Profusion beautyberry

The name says it all! If you first encounter this shrub in the spring, you may wonder why anyone would plant it. Once you see the berries that appear in the fall, you'll understand. This beautyberry's purplish pink summer flowers are quite subtle, but the berries that appear in the fall are far from subtle. Their intense violet color is a stand-out in any garden setting.

Plant Type:	Shrub	**Height:**	6'
Season of Interest:	Summer, Fall	**Spread:**	6'
Flower Color:	Purplish pink	**USDA Hardiness Zone:**	5-8
Exposure:	Full sun, Part sun	**Wildlife Attractions:**	Birds

Yuletide camellia

flowering quince

Camellia sasanqua 'Yuletide'
Yuletide camellia

'Yuletide' has showy red blooms with golden yellow centers that appear just in time for the holiday season. This evergreen shrub is great for hedges, privacy screenings, or containers. It performs best in acidic soils.

Plant Type:	Shrub	**Height:**	8-10'
Season of Interest:	Fall, Winter	**Spread:**	6'
Flower Color:	Red	**USDA Hardiness Zone:**	7-10
Exposure:	Full sun, Part sun	**Wildlife Attractions:**	Birds

Chaenomeles speciosa 'Scarlet Storm'
flowering quince

Thornless, this quince features large, camellia-like flowers that bloom in early spring. 'Scarlet Storm' is perfect for a landscape border, cutting garden, or container. It does not produce fruit. Very drought tolerant and deer resistant.

Plant Type:	Shrub	**Height:**	5'
Season of Interest:	Spring	**Spread:**	4'
Flower Color:	Bright red	**USDA Hardiness Zone:**	5-9
Exposure:	Full sun, Part sun	**Wildlife Attractions:**	Bees

Arctic Fire red twig dogwood

Harry Lauder's walking stick

Cornus sericea 'Arctic Fire'
Arctic Fire red twig dogwood

'Arctic Fire' has great fall color but is best known for its red bark, which becomes more visible once the plant sheds its leaves in fall. The red color intensifies as the temperatures dip. To maintain the best color, prune out the oldest branches in the early spring, as the color is most intense on the newest growth.

Plant Type:	Shrub	Height:	3-4'
Season of Interest:	Fall, Winter	Spread:	3-4'
Flower Color:	White	USDA Hardiness Zone:	3-7
Exposure:	Full sun, Part sun	Wildlife Attractions:	Birds

Corylus avellana 'Contorta'
Harry Lauder's walking stick

This shrub looks best in winter, once it drops its leaves to reveal its contorted and twisted branch structure. In the spring, yellow male catkins appear that resemble skinny, fuzzy caterpillars hanging from the branches. 'Contorta' is best used as specimen planting.

Plant Type:	Shrub	Height:	6'
Season of Interest:	Winter, Spring	Spread:	6'
Flower Color:	Yellow	USDA Hardiness Zone:	4-8
Exposure:	Full sun, Part sun	Wildlife Attractions:	None

Bearberry Cotoneaster

lilac daphne

Cotoneaster dammeri
Bearberry Cotoneaster

Bearberry Cotoneaster possesses glossy green foliage that provides winter interest in reddish-purple hues. An extremely fast grower, it is one of the best providers of evergreen ground coverage. Its best use is for hillside and slopes, planted in masses, and it spreads quickly due to its free-rooting quality. The flowers are insignificant. Deer resistant.

Plant Type:	Shrub	**Height:**	1'
Season of Interest:	Year-round	**Spread:**	6'
Flower Color:	White	**USDA Hardiness Zone:**	5–8
Exposure:	Full sun, Part sun	**Wildlife Attractions:**	Birds

Daphne genkwa
lilac daphne

This shrub's bare branches are covered in lavender blooms that have a soft fragrance in early to mid-spring. Small in stature, this daphne is perfect for small spaces.

Plant Type:	Shrub	**Height:**	3'
Season of Interest:	Spring	**Spread:**	3'
Flower Color:	Lavender	**USDA Hardiness Zone:**	5–7
Exposure:	Full sun, Part sun, Part shade	**Wildlife Attractions:**	Butterflies

Summer Ice Caucasian daphne

Chinese quinine

Daphne × transatlantica 'Summer Ice'
Summer Ice Caucasian daphne

Wonderfully fragrant and semi-evergreen (in our Zone 8B) with champagne-colored flowers, 'Summer Ice' blooms from April until November for us! Its leaves are edged with pale yellow. In order to best access its fragrance, plant 'Summer Ice' near an entranceway or along a walkway. It is low maintenance and resistant to deer.

Plant Type:	Shrub	Height:	4'
Season of Interest:	Spring, Summer, Fell	Spread:	6'
Flower Color:	Blush pink	USDA Hardiness Zone:	6-8
Exposure:	Full sun, Part shade	Wildlife Attractions:	Bees, Butterflies

Dichroa febrifuga
Chinese quinine

This acid-loving evergreen shrub is in the same family as hydrangeas. Its most notable trait is its blue flowers, which contain neodymium, the same element that creates the color in our lavender glass *Reeds*. The flowers are followed by berries of a similar color. It gets its common name from its use in traditional Chinese medicine.

Plant Type:	Shrub	Height:	4-6'
Season of Interest:	Summer, Winter	Spread:	4-6'
Flower Color:	Lavender	USDA Hardiness Zone:	8-10
Exposure:	Full sun, Part sun	Wildlife Attractions:	Bees, Birds, Butterflies

rice paper shrub

tree ivy

Edgeworthia chrysantha
rice paper shrub

This *Edgeworthia* has extremely fragrant clusters of golden yellow flowers in the late winter. The blooms are quite striking against the bare branches.

Plant Type:	Shrub	**Height:**	8'
Season of Interest:	Winter	**Spread:**	8'
Flower Color:	Yellow	**USDA Hardiness Zone:**	7–10
Exposure:	Part sun, Part shade	**Wildlife Attractions:**	Hummingbirds

Fatshedera lizei
tree ivy

This evergreen, vine-like shrub is a cross between a fatsia and an ivy plant. It's great to add privacy to a space but needs support to grow upright. In the late fall, globular white flowers that look very tropical appear, adding to the interest of this species.

Plant Type:	Shrub	**Height:**	6-8'
Season of Interest:	Year-round	**Spread:**	6'
Flower Color:	White	**USDA Hardiness Zone:**	7-9
Exposure:	Part shade, Shade	**Wildlife Attractions:**	None

fatsia, Japanese fatsia

dwarf witchalder, dwarf fothergilla

Fatsia japonica
fatsia, Japanese fatsia

This tropical-looking, evergreen shrub performs best in shade. Attractive palmate leaves and drumstick-like flowers add to its appeal. Cut leaves look great in floral arrangements.

Plant Type:	Shrub	**Height:**	6'
Season of Interest:	Year-round	**Spread:**	6'
Flower Color:	Cream	**USDA Hardiness Zone:**	7-9
Exposure:	Part shade, Shade	**Wildlife Attractions:**	None

Fothergilla gardenii
dwarf witchalder, dwarf fothergilla

Dwarf fothergilla is a native American shrub that provides outstanding fall color and bears fragrant, bottlebrush-like flowers on a compact habit. This plant can be massed attractively in the landscape, be used as an accent, or even serve as a shrub border. It is rarely damaged by deer.

Plant Type:	Shrub	**Height:**	5'
Season of Interest:	Spring, Fall	**Spread:**	4'
Flower Color:	White	**USDA Hardiness Zone:**	5-9
Exposure:	Full sun, Part sun	**Wildlife Attractions:**	Bees, Butterflies

Japanese witch hazel

Bluebird lacecap hydrangea

Hamamelis japonica 'Shibamichi Red'
Japanese witch hazel

A cherry-red, late winter bloomer, this variety has flowers that are subtly fragrant and ribbon-like. The fall color of the foliage is exceptional: shades of yellow, red, and purple. 'Shibamichi Red' is an excellent variety to display in groupings but can also work well as a specimen or accent shrub. It is not commonly damaged by deer.

Plant Type:	Shrub	**Height:**	10–15'
Season of Interest:	Fall, Winter, Spring	**Spread:**	10–15'
Flower Color:	Red	**USDA Hardiness Zone:**	5–8
Exposure:	Full sun, Part sun, Part shade	**Wildlife Attractions:**	None

Hydrangea macrophylla ssp. *serrata* 'Bluebird'
Bluebird lacecap hydrangea

This lacecap hydrangea has delicate blooms that become a more intense blue tone as the soil acidity increases.

Plant Type:	Shrub	**Height:**	4'
Season of Interest:	Summer, Fall	**Spread:**	4'
Flower Color:	Light blue–light pink	**USDA Hardiness Zone:**	5–8
Exposure:	Part sun, Part shade	**Wildlife Attractions:**	None

Blue Deckle lacecap hydrangea

Yae-No-Amacha lacecap hydrangea

Hydrangea macrophylla ssp. *serrata* 'Blue Deckle'
Blue Deckle lacecap hydrangea

Similar in appearance to 'Bluebird', but petals have a subtle jagged edge.

Plant Type:	Shrub	Height:	4'
Season of Interest:	Summer, Fall	Spread:	4'
Flower Color:	Light blue–light pink	USDA Hardiness Zone:	5–9
Exposure:	Part sun, Part shade	Wildlife Attractions:	None

Hydrangea macrophylla ssp. *serrata* 'Yae-No-Amacha'
Yae-No-Amacha lacecap hydrangea

'Yae-No-Amacha' is similar to the other lacecap hydrangeas but with double petals.

Plant Type:	Shrub	Height:	4'
Season of Interest:	Summer, Fall	Spread:	4'
Flower Color:	Light blue–light pink	USDA Hardiness Zone:	5–9
Exposure:	Part sun, Part shade	Wildlife Attractions:	None

Limelight panicle hydrangea   oakleaf hydrangea

Hydrangea paniculata 'Limelight'
Limelight panicle hydrangea

'Limelight' has dense, conical clusters of flowers that appear mid- to late summer and hold well into fall. You can allow the dry flower heads to persist into winter to add an additional season of interest. This panicle hydrangea is much larger in size than the other hydrangeas you will find in the garden, making it a highlight of the late summer season.

Plant Type:	Shrub	**Height:**	10'
Season of Interest:	Summer, Fall, Winter	**Spread:**	9'
Flower Color:	White–lime green	**USDA Hardiness Zone:**	4–8
Exposure:	Full sun, Part sun, Part shade	**Wildlife Attractions:**	None

Hydrangea quercifolia 'Pee Wee'
oakleaf hydrangea

Oakleaf hydrangeas get their name from their oak-shaped leaves that make them easily recognizable compared to other hydrangeas. 'Pee Wee' has great fall color, beautiful flower heads, and interesting peeling bark.

Plant Type:	Shrub	**Height:**	5'
Season of Interest:	Summer, Fall, Winter	**Spread:**	6'
Flower Color:	White	**USDA Hardiness Zone:**	5–8
Exposure:	Part Shade	**Wildlife Attractions:**	None

dwarf mountain hydrangea

boxleaf honeysuckle

Hydrangea serrata 'Tiny Tuff Stuff'
dwarf mountain hydrangea

'Tiny Tuff Stuff' is most notable for its small stature but also puts on a great show in late spring to early summer while in bloom. Clusters of semi-double blue flowers contrast beautifully with the deep red blush on the green foliage. Great for small gardens.

Plant Type:	Shrub	**Height:**	2'
Season of Interest:	Year-round	**Spread:**	2'
Flower Color:	Light blue–light pink	**USDA Hardiness Zone:**	5-9
Exposure:	Full sun, Part sun, Part shade	**Wildlife Attractions:**	None

Lonicera nitida
boxleaf honeysuckle

An evergreen and very dense shrub, boxleaf honeysuckle produces dark purple fruit that appears in late summer. Foliage is glossy with a rounded leaf shape and will take on a purple hue in the winter. This plant makes an excellent ground cover, especially for slopes or hillsides. Deer resistant.

Plant Type:	Shrub	**Height:**	5'
Season of Interest:	Year-round	**Spread:**	4-7'
Flower Color:	White	**USDA Hardiness Zone:**	6-9
Exposure:	Full sun, Part sun, Part shade	**Wildlife Attractions:**	Birds

privet honeysuckle

Japanese mahonia

Lonicera pileata
privet honeysuckle

Though smaller in stature than *Lonicera nitida*, privet honeysuckle features longer and wider leaves, and the habit is more horizontal. The evergreen foliage matched with the graceful spreading habit makes privet honeysuckle a wonderful go-to ground cover. The fruit is amethyst in color, appearing in summer after the flowers have senesced. Deer resistant.

Plant Type:	Shrub	Height:	2-3'
Season of Interest:	Year-round	Spread:	8'
Flower Color:	Yellow-white	USDA Hardiness Zone:	6-9
Exposure:	Full sun, Part sun	Wildlife Attractions:	Birds

Mahonia japonica
Japanese mahonia

Hummingbirds can be seen frequenting this evergreen shrub, feeding on its fragrant lemon yellow winter blooms. The flowers are followed by bunches of grape-like bluish black berries. This mahonia is great in a woodland garden, especially in mass. It spreads by suckering. Flowers and fruit are more abundant in larger groupings as compared to singular plants. The leathery, glossy green leaves have sharp points, making this good for use as a barricade.

Plant Type:	Shrub	Height:	6-10'
Season of Interest:	Year-round	Spread:	6-10'
Flower Color:	Yellow	USDA Hardiness Zone:	6-8
Exposure:	Part sun, Part shade, Shade	Wildlife Attractions:	Bees, Hummingbirds

Brouwer's Beauty lily-of-the-valley shrub

Prelude lily-of-the-valley shrub

Pieris japonica 'Brouwer's Beauty'
Brouwer's Beauty lily-of-the-valley shrub

'Brouwer's Beauty' has deep red buds that reveal dainty chains of bell-shaped white flowers in early spring. This evergreen shrub's new growth appears yellow before darkening to a deep green. Beautiful either stand-alone or in a grouping.

Plant Type:	Shrub	**Height:**	5'
Season of Interest:	Winter, Spring	**Spread:**	4'
Flower Color:	White	**USDA Hardiness Zone:**	4–8
Exposure:	Full sun, Part sun, Part shade	**Wildlife Attractions:**	None

Pieris japonica 'Prelude'
Prelude lily-of-the-valley shrub

'Prelude' is a dwarf variety that reaches only 2 feet high. Similar to 'Brouwer's Beauty', chains of bell-shaped white flowers appear in spring. Great for small gardens or in mass.

Plant Type:	Shrub	**Height:**	2'
Season of Interest:	Year-round	**Spread:**	3'
Flower Color:	White	**USDA Hardiness Zone:**	5–8
Exposure:	Full sun, Part sun, Part shade	**Wildlife Attractions:**	None

Japanese mock orange

alpine plum yew

Pittosporum tobira 'Wheeler's Dwarf'
Japanese mock orange

Foundation planting as an understory shrub or hedging is a common use for this plant. It benefits from a yearly shearing to encourage a tidier appearance. Salt tolerance makes pittosporum an ideal beach plant. Flowers are very fragrant.

Plant Type:	Shrub	**Height:**	2–3'
Season of Interest:	Year-round	**Spread:**	4–5'
Flower Color:	White-yellow	**USDA Hardiness Zone:**	8–11
Exposure:	Full sun, Part sun, Part shade	**Wildlife Attractions:**	None

Podocarpus lawrencei 'Blue Gem'
alpine plum yew

We use this as a massing ground cover and chose 'Blue Gem' for its evergreen blue-green color, red new growth, and fine texture. It is drought tolerant once established.

Plant Type:	Shrub	**Height:**	2'
Season of Interest:	Year-round	**Spread:**	2'
Flower Color:	None	**USDA Hardiness Zone:**	7–9
Exposure:	Full sun, Part sun	**Wildlife Attractions:**	Birds

Mount Vernon cherry laurel

Black Sport rhododendron

Prunus laurocerasus 'Mount Vernon'
Mount Vernon cherry laurel

With evergreen foliage and a tidy, nonaggressive dwarf habit, this plant makes an exceptional ground cover. 'Mount Vernon' is tough. It can withstand drought, dry shade, and even poor soil conditions.

Plant Type:	Shrub	**Height:**	2'
Season of Interest:	Year-round	**Spread:**	5'
Flower Color:	Yellow-white	**USDA Hardiness Zone:**	6–9
Exposure:	Full sun, Part sun, Part shade, Shade	**Wildlife Attractions:**	None

Rhododendron 'Black Sport'
Black Sport rhododendron

Flowers are dark purple-magenta with a deep black-red blotch on the upper lobe. The foliage is deep green and grows upward, often showing the underside of the leaf.

Plant Type:	Shrub	**Height:**	6–7'
Season of Interest:	Spring, Summer	**Spread:**	5–6'
Flower Color:	Dark purple-red	**USDA Hardiness Zone:**	6–8
Exposure:	Full sun, Part sun	**Wildlife Attractions:**	Butterflies

Cunningham White rhododendron   Dreamland rhododendron

Rhododendron 'Cunningham White'
Cunningham White rhododendron

It is the best rootstock for grafted plants and is used throughout the world for grafting. It is resistant to root weevils and is a great woodland perennial due to its resistance to deer.

Plant Type:	Shrub	**Height:**	4–6'
Season of Interest:	Spring, Summer	**Spread:**	4–6'
Flower Color:	Blush pink buds open to white	**USDA Hardiness Zone:**	6–8
Exposure:	Full sun, Part sun	**Wildlife Attractions:**	Butterflies

Rhododendron 'Dreamland'
Dreamland rhododendron

'Dreamland' is an attractive, dense, evergreen shrub with large trusses of showy trumpet-shaped soft-pink flowers bordered with deeper pink edges. A prolific bloomer.

Plant Type:	Shrub	**Height:**	4'
Season of Interest:	Spring, Summer	**Spread:**	4'
Flower Color:	Pink	**USDA Hardiness Zone:**	6–8
Exposure:	Full sun, Part sun, Part shade	**Wildlife Attractions:**	Bees

Ramapo rhododendron

Chihuly floribunda rose

Rhododendron 'Ramapo'
Ramapo rhododendron

'Ramapo' is a good choice for small patio gardens, borders, and mass planting in the landscape. This compact, evergreen shrub is a profuse bloomer that provides quite the show in mid-spring.

Plant Type:	Shrub	**Height:**	3'
Season of Interest:	Spring, Summer	**Spread:**	3'
Flower Color:	Violet	**USDA Hardiness Zone:**	4–8
Exposure:	Full sun, Part sun, Part shade	**Wildlife Attractions:**	Bees, Butterflies

Rosa floribunda 'Chihuly'
Chihuly floribunda rose

Extremely vibrant 3-to-4-inch blooms appear in late spring. A real showstopper. Benefits from regular fertilization.

Plant Type:	Shrub	**Height:**	4'
Season of Interest:	Spring, Summer	**Spread:**	4'
Flower Color:	Yellow to orange	**USDA Hardiness Zone:**	6–10
Exposure:	Full sun, Part sun	**Wildlife Attractions:**	Bees, Butterflies

Icy Drift carpet rose

Black Lace elderberry

Rosa 'Icy Drift'
Icy Drift carpet rose

Small white blooms cover this rose from late spring to the first frost. Benefits from a heavy pruning to open up the shrub, along with dead wooding.

Plant Type:	Shrub	**Height:**	2'
Season of Interest:	Spring, Summer, Fall	**Spread:**	3'
Flower Color:	White	**USDA Hardiness Zone:**	5-10
Exposure:	Full sun, Part sun	**Wildlife Attractions:**	Bees, Butterflies

Sambucus nigra 'Black Lace'
Black Lace elderberry

The deep purple foliage of 'Black Lace' has a feather-like texture. Paired with its open branch structure, this shrub has a light and airy feel in the landscape. This is an exceptional specimen plant. *Sambucus nigra* is a deer-resistant plant.

Plant Type:	Shrub	**Height:**	6-8'
Season of Interest:	Spring, Summer	**Spread:**	6-8'
Flower Color:	Creamy pink	**USDA Hardiness Zone:**	4-7
Exposure:	Full sun	**Wildlife Attractions:**	Birds

dwarf sweetbox

Delavay's schefflera

Sarcococca hookeriana var. *humilis*
dwarf sweetbox

Small, fragrant flowers cover this compact shrub beginning in late winter. Evergreen foliage makes this a nice addition for year-round structure in a shade garden.

Plant Type:	Shrub	**Height:**	2'
Season of Interest:	Winter, Spring	**Spread:**	2-3'
Flower Color:	White	**USDA Hardiness Zone:**	4-9
Exposure:	Part shade, Shade	**Wildlife Attractions:**	None

Schefflera delavayi
Delavay's schefflera

Evergreen. Blooms in fall with sprays of tiny white flowers. New foliage growth appears tawny and fuzz covered. Its umbrella habit is created by the glossy dark green leaves at the top of the trunk. Ideal for temperate gardens.

Plant Type:	Shrub	**Height:**	8'
Season of Interest:	Spring	**Spread:**	8'
Flower Color:	Ivory	**USDA Hardiness Zone:**	7-9
Exposure:	Part sun, Part shade	**Wildlife Attractions:**	None

Marie's doublefile viburnum

paperbark maple

Viburnum plicatum f. *tomentosum* 'Mariesii'
Marie's doublefile viburnum

Doublefile viburnum is considered an easy-maintenance shrub. It looks best when displayed in mass. Attractive lateral branching is exposed in the winter. Beautiful hydrangea-like blooms in the spring with a fall rebloom. Excellent fall color. Deer resistant and salt tolerant.

Plant Type:	Shrub	**Height:**	12'
Season of Interest:	Year-round	**Spread:**	10'
Flower Color:	White	**USDA Hardiness Zone:**	4–8
Exposure:	Full sun, Part sun	**Wildlife Attractions:**	Birds

TREES

Acer griseum
paperbark maple

Acer griseum is a tree well suited for smaller gardens, with the major interest being the paper-like, peeling bark that occurs year-round. In addition, leaves turn to shades of pumpkin orange, buttery gold, and brick red in the fall. It is also tolerable of compacted soils.

Plant Type:	Tree, deciduous	**Height:**	18'
Season of Interest:	Year-round	**Spread:**	15'
Flower Color:	Insignificant	**USDA Hardiness Zone:**	5–8
Exposure:	Full sun, Part sun, Part shade	**Wildlife Attractions:**	Birds

red weeping cut-leaf Japanese maple

coral bark Japanese maple

Acer palmatum 'Dissectum Atropurpureum'
red weeping cut-leaf Japanese maple

'Dissectum Atropurpureum' has feather-like deep burgundy leaves that add both texture and color to a landscape. Additionally, this ornamental tree has a weeping habit that makes it a strong specimen.

Plant Type:	Tree, deciduous	**Height:**	6–8'
Season of Interest:	Spring, Summer, Fall	**Spread:**	6–8'
Flower Color:	Insignificant	**USDA Hardiness Zone:**	5–8
Exposure:	Full sun, Part sun, Part shade	**Wildlife Attractions:**	Birds

Acer palmatum 'Sango Kaku'
coral bark Japanese maple

'Sango Kaku' is a prime example of multi-seasonal interest. It provides excellent color contrast in the winter with its coral-red bark, vibrant golden to orange fall color, and beautiful chartreuse-colored leaves in spring and summer. It's a focal point in the garden no matter the time of year.

Plant Type:	Tree, deciduous	**Height:**	10–25'
Season of Interest:	Year-round	**Spread:**	15–20'
Flower Color:	Reddish-purple	**USDA Hardiness Zone:**	5–8
Exposure:	Full sun, Part sun, Part shade	**Wildlife Attractions:**	Birds

golden full moon maple

Oregon Blue Lawson's cypress

Acer shirasawanum 'Aureum'
golden full moon maple

This maple has incredibly brilliant foliage color throughout the year, from bright lemon to chartreuse, and eventually to orange and red in fall. Ornamental red samaras also provide interest into the summer months. The tree's framework provides winter interest and makes this full moon maple a great selection for containers.

Plant Type:	Tree, deciduous	**Height:**	8'
Season of Interest:	Year-round	**Spread:**	7'
Flower Color:	None	**USDA Hardiness Zone:**	5–8
Exposure:	Part shade	**Wildlife Attractions:**	Birds

Chamaecyparis lawsoniana 'Oregon Blue'
Oregon Blue Lawson's cypress

This tree looks great with broad-leaved evergreens. It makes a good screen that will act as a sound barrier as well as providing privacy. Great for Christmas and floral arrangements, the foliage is aromatic and soft and lasts well when cut.

Plant Type:	Tree, conifer	**Height:**	30'
Season of Interest:	Year-round	**Spread:**	12'
Flower Color:	None	**USDA Hardiness Zone:**	5–8
Exposure:	Full sun, Part sun	**Wildlife Attractions:**	Birds

weeping Alaskan cedar

slender hinoki cypress

Chamaecyparis nootkatensis 'Glauca Pendula'
weeping Alaskan cedar

This is a beautiful specimen tree that has an upright and extremely narrow form. The true charm is the whimsy of swooping branches, weeping foliage, and curving trunk.

Plant Type:	Tree, conifer	**Height:**	30'+
Season of Interest:	Year-round	**Spread:**	10-15'
Flower Color:	None	**USDA Hardiness Zone:**	5-7
Exposure:	Full sun, Part sun	**Wildlife Attractions:**	Birds

Chamaecyparis obtusa 'Gracilis'
slender hinoki cypress

The slender hinoki cypress is the ideal evergreen for smaller gardens and narrow spaces. This tree grows in a columnar/pyramidal form and branches are fan-like, creating an elegant statement for borders and backdrops. As a slow-growing species, this could also work well as a container plant. There are no serious insect or disease problems.

Plant Type:	Tree, conifer	**Height:**	8-15'
Season of Interest:	Year-round	**Spread:**	4-6'
Flower Color:	None	**USDA Hardiness Zone:**	4-8
Exposure:	Full sun, Part sun, Part shade	**Wildlife Attractions:**	Birds

Celestial dogwood

Black Dragon Japanese cedar

Cornus rutgersensis 'Celestial'
Celestial dogwood

'Celestial' is known for its vigorous habit as well as its resistance to anthracnose and dogwood borer. It is a profuse bloomer with large-bracted flowers, a definite improvement on the flowers of a true dogwood. Prefers moist, acidic soils and benefits from a 2-to-4-inch mulch layer in the summer months.

Plant Type:	Tree, deciduous	**Height:**	14–18'
Season of Interest:	Spring, Summer, Fall	**Spread:**	12–15'
Flower Color:	White, maturing to pink	**USDA Hardiness Zone:**	5–9
Exposure:	Full sun, Part sun, Part shade	**Wildlife Attractions:**	Butterflies

Cryptomeria japonica 'Black Dragon'
Black Dragon Japanese cedar

A pyramidal-shaped evergreen with a slow growth rate, Black Dragon Japanese cedar is excellent to use as a foundation planting around buildings. It also makes a beautiful backdrop or screen. Black Dragon Japanese cedar is drought tolerant once established.

Plant Type:	Tree or shrub, conifer	**Height:**	10–12'
Season of Interest:	Year-round	**Spread:**	4–6'
Flower Color:	None	**USDA Hardiness Zone:**	6–9
Exposure:	Full sun, Part sun	**Wildlife Attractions:**	Birds

Sonoma dove tree, handkerchief tree

Shademaster thornless honeylocust

Davidia involucrata 'Sonoma'
Sonoma dove tree, handkerchief tree

Dove trees have very showy white pairs of bracts in the spring, which evoke images of dove wings or a handkerchief. These pairs surround a single round bloom, which itself is not showy in nature. The flowers are followed by kumquat-sized nuts that appear in fall and are held into the winter.

Plant Type:	Tree, deciduous	Height:	20–40'
Season of Interest:	Spring, Fall	Spread:	20–40'
Flower Color:	Brown with large white bracts	USDA Hardiness Zone:	6–8
Exposure:	Full sun, Part sun, Part shade	Wildlife Attractions:	Butterflies

Gleditsia triacanthos var. *inermis* 'Shademaster'
Shademaster thornless honeylocust

'Shademaster' possesses dark green foliage that turns golden in the fall. This podless variety (requires little raking maintenance!), with a vase-like growth habit, is one that many horticulturists claim to be their favorite. Strongly growing with small leaflets, it provides filtered, soft shade. Drought and salt tolerant.

Plant Type:	Tree, deciduous	Height:	50'
Season of Interest:	Spring, Summer, Fall	Spread:	35'
Flower Color:	None	USDA Hardiness Zone:	5–8
Exposure:	Full sun	Wildlife Attractions:	Birds

Bracken's Brown Beauty magnolia

Teddy Bear magnolia

Magnolia grandiflora 'Bracken's Brown Beauty'
Bracken's Brown Beauty magnolia

A cold-hardy cultivar and one of the very best selections due to its dense, compact form and cold-hardiness, 'Bracken's Brown Beauty' has evergreen, leathery dark green leaves with rusty brown undersides and undulating edges. The flowers are showy and extremely fragrant. It drops fewer leaves than many of the other cultivars.

Plant Type:	Tree, broad-leaved evergreen	**Height:**	40'
Season of Interest:	Year-round	**Spread:**	30'
Flower Color:	None	**USDA Hardiness Zone:**	6-9
Exposure:	Full sun, Part sun	**Wildlife Attractions:**	Birds

Magnolia grandiflora 'Teddy Bear'
Teddy Bear magnolia

'Teddy Bear' is a very dense and compact magnolia. Its evergreen, two-tone leaves are a deep, glossy green on top, while the underside sports a reddish-brown felt. In late spring to early summer, very large cream flowers appear. This tree is suited for a privacy screening but also makes a great specimen.

Plant Type:	Tree, broad-leaved evergreen	**Height:**	20'
Season of Interest:	Year-round	**Spread:**	12'
Flower Color:	Cream	**USDA Hardiness Zone:**	7-9
Exposure:	Full sun	**Wildlife Attractions:**	Birds

weeping Colorado blue spruce

Wintergreen umbrella pine

Picea pungens 'Glauca Pendula'
weeping Colorado blue spruce

Due to the striking quality of the blue foliage and its habit, the weeping Colorado blue spruce can serve as a specimen or focal point in the garden. It also looks great in mass plantings. Very adaptable and drought tolerant.

Plant Type:	Tree or shrub, conifer	**Height:**	4'
Season of Interest:	Year-round	**Spread:**	8'
Flower Color:	None	**USDA Hardiness Zone:**	3-7
Exposure:	Full sun	**Wildlife Attractions:**	None

Sciadopitys verticillata 'Wintergreen'
Wintergreen umbrella pine

Texturally, this is one of the most interesting conifers one will find. Best used as a specimen or accent tree. New growth in the late spring is a striking lime green before maturing to a deep forest green. Interesting cones add to this conifer's appeal.

Plant Type:	Tree, conifer	**Height:**	20-30'
Season of Interest:	Year-round	**Spread:**	15-20'
Flower Color:	None	**USDA Hardiness Zone:**	5-7
Exposure:	Full sun, Part sun	**Wildlife Attractions:**	Birds

Japanese stewartia   spreading English yew

Stewartia pseudocamellia
Japanese stewartia

This small-statured tree has multi-seasonal interest. In early summer, white blooms that resemble camellias appear. When fall arrives, *Stewartia pseudocamellia* turns brilliant shades of orange and rusty reds. Winter highlights the tree's unique bark and its interesting but subtle branch pattern.

Plant Type:	Tree, deciduous	**Height:**	25'
Season of Interest:	Year-round	**Spread:**	12'
Flower Color:	White	**USDA Hardiness Zone:**	5–8
Exposure:	Part sun	**Wildlife Attractions:**	Birds

Taxus baccata 'Repandens'
spreading English yew

This yew works well as a foundation planting, especially in mass. It prefers well-drained soil and can withstand drought once established. Bright red arils surround a single seed cone. Multiple parts of this tree are poisonous, so place appropriately in the landscape.

Plant Type:	Shrub, conifer	**Height:**	4'
Season of Interest:	Year-round	**Spread:**	10'
Flower Color:	None	**USDA Hardiness Zone:**	5–9
Exposure:	Full sun	**Wildlife Attractions:**	None

dwarf Japanese yew

western red cedar

Taxus cuspidata 'Nana'
dwarf Japanese yew

With a more upright habit than the spreading variety, the dwarf variety is well suited to smaller spaces.

Plant Type:	Shrub, conifer	**Height:**	3'
Season of Interest:	Year-round	**Spread:**	6'
Flower Color:	None	**USDA Hardiness Zone:**	3-7
Exposure:	Full sun	**Wildlife Attractions:**	None

Thuja plicata 'Atrovirens'
western red cedar

'Atrovirens' is a smaller variety of cedar that makes it great for screening in a small garden. With its aromatic foliage and reddish-brown bark, it's a good addition to many landscapes.

Plant Type:	Tree, conifer	**Height:**	30-40'
Season of Interest:	Year-round	**Spread:**	15-20'
Flower Color:	None	**USDA Hardiness Zone:**	5-7
Exposure:	Full sun	**Wildlife Attractions:**	Birds

chocolate vine, fiveleaf akebia

Arabella ground cover clematis

VINES

Akebia quinata
chocolate vine, fiveleaf akebia

Akebia quinata is a deciduous vine that climbs by twining. Fragrant, deep burgundy, almost brown, flowers appear in spring. Purple fruit pods form in fall. Performs best in full sun but tolerates shade. Deer tolerant. May be invasive in parts of the country.

Plant Type:	Vine	**Height:**	20-40'
Season of Interest:	Spring, Summer, Fall	**Spread:**	5-10'
Flower Color:	Burgundy	**USDA Hardiness Zone:**	4-8
Exposure:	Full sun, Part sun, Part shade	**Wildlife Attractions:**	Bees

Clematis 'Arabella'
Arabella ground cover clematis

This clematis is a prolific bloomer and one of the very few ground cover forms. Also great for containers. Grow in moist, well-drained soil, paying special attention to keep roots cool by mulching.

Plant Type:	Vine, Perennial	**Height:**	3-6'
Season of Interest:	Spring, Summer	**Spread:**	3-6'
Flower Color:	Dark lavender	**USDA Hardiness Zone:**	4-8
Exposure:	Full sun, Part sun	**Wildlife Attractions:**	Bees

evergreen clematis

Sweet Autumn clematis

Clematis armandii
evergreen clematis

Extremely fragrant white flowers cover this vine in March. Long and slender, evergreen leaves add to this vine's appeal. Drought tolerant once well established. Performs better when the root area is shaded by surrounding shrubs or heavily mulched.

Plant Type:	Vine	Height:	20–25'
Season of Interest:	Year-round	Spread:	10–15'
Flower Color:	White	USDA Hardiness Zone:	7–9
Exposure:	Full sun, Part sun, Part shade	Wildlife Attractions:	None

Clematis ternifolia 'Sweet Autumn'
Sweet Autumn clematis

Very fragrant white flowers cover this vine in late summer or early fall. Blooms on new wood. Prune hard after blooming or in early spring.

Plant Type:	Vine	Height:	15–30'
Season of Interest:	Summer, Fall	Spread:	15–30'
Flower Color:	White	USDA Hardiness Zone:	5–9
Exposure:	Full sun, Part sun, Part shade	Wildlife Attractions:	None

Cathedral Gem sausage vine

China Blue sausage vine

Holboellia coriacea 'Cathedral Gem'
Cathedral Gem sausage vine

White buds open to mauve flowers. Extremely fragrant blooms. This plant has glossy, evergreen foliage and edible, sausage-shaped fruit.

Plant Type:	Vine	**Height:**	25'
Season of Interest:	Year-round	**Spread:**	10–15'
Flower Color:	Mauve	**USDA Hardiness Zone:**	7–10
Exposure:	Full sun, Part sun, Part shade	**Wildlife Attractions:**	Hummingbirds

Holboellia coriacea 'China Blue'
China Blue sausage vine

Fragrant flowers bloom in early spring. This plant has glossy, evergreen foliage and edible, sausage-shaped fruit.

Plant Type:	Vine	**Height:**	25'
Season of Interest:	Year-round	**Spread:**	10–15'
Flower Color:	White	**USDA Hardiness Zone:**	7–10
Exposure:	Full sun, Part sun, Part shade	**Wildlife Attractions:**	None

evergreen climbing hydrangea

Serotina honeysuckle

Hydrangea integrifolia
evergreen climbing hydrangea

Evergreen and climbing by way of aerial roots, this vine produces large, globular flower buds that break open to reveal gorgeous, lacy white blooms in early summer. It's vigorous, great for covering walls, and does surprisingly well in part shade. The new growth is coppery red in tone, while the older growth is lush dark green.

Plant Type:	Vine	**Height:**	40'
Season of Interest:	Year-round	**Spread:**	20'
Flower Color:	White	**USDA Hardiness Zone:**	7–9
Exposure:	Full sun, Part sun, Part shade	**Wildlife Attractions:**	Bees, Butterflies

Lonicera periclymenum 'Serotina'
Serotina honeysuckle

An easy-to-grow, reliable, and self-climbing vine. Very fragrant and floriferous, with a long blooming season. Flower clusters are dark pink and creamy white. Red berries form after the flowers have senesced. Semi-evergreen in milder climates. Deer resistant.

Plant Type:	Vine	**Height:**	20'
Season of Interest:	Summer, Fall	**Spread:**	15'
Flower Color:	Pink and white	**USDA Hardiness Zone:**	5–9
Exposure:	Full sun, Part sun, Part shade	**Wildlife Attractions:**	Bees, Butterflies, Hummingbirds

Major Wheeler trumpet honeysuckle

confederate jasmine

Lonicera sempervirens 'Major Wheeler'
Major Wheeler trumpet honeysuckle

Trumpet honeysuckle is a major hummingbird magnet that is vigorous and fast growing. 'Major Wheeler' thrives in humidity and is mildew resistant.

Plant Type:	Vine	**Height:**	8'
Season of Interest:	Spring, Summer, Fall	**Spread:**	10'
Flower Color:	Crimson	**USDA Hardiness Zone:**	5–9
Exposure:	Full sun, Part sun	**Wildlife Attractions:**	Butterflies, Hummingbirds, Larger birds

Trachelospermum jasminoides
confederate jasmine

Intense and attractive fragrance with clusters of showy, star-shaped flowers and glossy green leaves. Climbs by twining and serves as a good wall or fence vine. Fast growing. Evergreen in milder climates.

Plant Type:	Vine	**Height:**	6'
Season of Interest:	Year-round	**Spread:**	6'
Flower Color:	White	**USDA Hardiness Zone:**	8–10
Exposure:	Full sun, Part sun, Part shade	**Wildlife Attractions:**	Bees

Japanese wisteria

Kentucky wisteria

Wisteria floribunda 'Cypress Blue'
Japanese wisteria

This Japanese native puts on a show in the spring when it blooms. Lavender clusters of flowers can be up to 3 feet in length. It grows quickly and can cover a large area. Ensure you grow it on a very sturdy structure, because it can get quite heavy over time.

Plant Type:	Vine	**Height:**	30'
Season of Interest:	Spring, Summer	**Spread:**	30'
Flower Color:	Lavender	**USDA Hardiness Zone:**	5-9
Exposure:	Full sun, Part sun	**Wildlife Attractions:**	Birds

Wisteria macrostachya 'Aunt Dee'
Kentucky wisteria

Later blooming than the Japanese varieties and hardier with showier blooms than the American varieties (*frutescens*), 'Aunt Dee' is highly fragrant and dangling with lilac flower clusters. Foliage is compound. Best if trained on a very strong fence or pergola.

Plant Type:	Vine	**Height:**	25'
Season of Interest:	Spring, Summer	**Spread:**	25'
Flower Color:	Lavender	**USDA Hardiness Zone:**	4-9
Exposure:	Full sun, Part sun	**Wildlife Attractions:**	Birds

Amber Herons, 2012

Black Herons, Black Eelgrass, and Niijima Float, 2012

Black Saguaros, 2012

Cattails and Niijima Floats, 2012

Citron Icicle Tower, 2012

Cobalt Reeds and Fiori, installed 2012

Double Turquoise Reeds, 2012

Green Hornets and Gold Waterdrops, 2013

Grey and White Eelgrass and Niijima Floats, 2012

Mexican Hat Tower,
2012

Neodymium Herons,
2012

Neodymium Reeds
and *Seal Pups*, 2012

Niijima Floats, 2012

Pacific Sun, 2011,
installed 2012

Red Reeds, 2012

Tiger Marlins, 2012

Turquoise Trumpets,
2012

Viola Crystal Tower,
2012

RESOURCES

Local Garden Center and Nursery Locator
www.gardens.com/local/garden-centers

American Public Gardens Association
www.publicgardens.org

National Wildlife Federation
www.nwf.org

Million Pollinator Garden Challenge
www.millionpollinatorgardens.org

U.S. Green Building Council
www.usgbc.org

Great Plant Picks
www.greatplantpicks.org

Armitage, Allan M. *Herbaceous Perennial Plants: A Treatise on Their Identification, Culture, and Garden Attributes.* 3rd ed. Champaign, Ill.: Stipes, 2008.

Dirr, Michael A. *Manual of Woody Landscape Plants: Their Identification, Ornamental Characteristics, Culture, Propagation and Uses.* 5th ed. Champaign, Ill.: Stipes, 1998.

Chihuly Garden and Glass
305 Harrison Street
Seattle, WA 98109
206.753.4940
info@chihulygardenandglass.com
www.chihulygardenandglass.com

Land Morphology
1512 Alaskan Way
Seattle, WA 98101
206.443.2120
info@landmorphology.com
www.landmorphology.com

For more information about Dale Chihuly, visit *www.chihuly.com*.

CHIHULY
GARDEN AND GLASS

COLOR FOR ALL SEASONS: FIELD GUIDE

Published by

CHIHULY™
WORKSHOP

P.O. Box 70856,
Seattle, WA 98127
800.574.7272
chihulyworkshop.com

ISBN: 978-1-57684-200-3

Design and Production
Goretti Kaomora, Bryson Chiu

Executive Consultants
Leslie Jackson Chihuly, Michelle Bufano, Diane Caillier

Copy Editor
Richard Slovak

Photography
Scott Mitchell Leen, Terry Rishel, Chelsea Runaas,
Chihuly Garden and Glass, Land Morphology

Typeset in Avenir Next, Linotype
Printed and Bound in China by Hing Yip Printing Co., Ltd.